New Economy – New Competition

New Economy – New Competition

The Rise of the Consumer?

David Asch and Brian Wolfe

First published 2001 by
PALGRAVE
Houndmills, Basingstoke, Hampshire RG21 6XS and
175 Fifth Avenue, New York, N.Y. 10010
Companies and representatives throughout the world

PALGRAVE is the new global academic imprint of
St. Martin's Press LLC Scholarly and Reference Division and
Palgrave Publishers Ltd (formerly Macmillan Press Ltd).

ISBN 0–333–77823–5

This book is printed on paper suitable for recycling and made from fully managed and sustained forest sources.

A catalogue record for this book is available from the British Library.

Library of Congress Cataloging-in-Publication Data

Asch, David, 1948–
    New economy—new competition : the rise of the consumer? / David Asch and Brian Wolfe
        p. cm.
    Includes bibliographical references and index.
    ISBN 0–333–77823–5
        1. Consumers—United States—Attitudes.
    2. Consumers—Europe—Attitudes. 3. Consumers'
    preferences—United States. 4. Consumers' preferences—
    Europe. 5. New Age consumers. 6. Consumer protection.
    7. Product safety. 8. Green marketing. 9. International
    trade—Sociological aspects. 10. Competition, International.
    I. Wolfe, Brian. II. Title.
HF5415.33.U6 A83 2000
    381.3'094—dc21   00–052419

10 9 8 7 6 5 4 3 2 1
10 09 08 07 06 05 04 03 02 01

Formatted by The Ascenders Partnership, Basingstoke

Printed and bound in Great Britain by
Creative Print and Design (Wales),
Ebbw Vale

*This book is dedicated to
Susan and Joy with love*

Contents

List of Figures and Tables

Foreword

The nature of business and competition has changed immeasurably over the past thirty years or so. In recent years the rate of change has accelerated and as we look forward it appears that increasing rates of change will be a phenomenon that all firms in competitive markets will have to address. The growth of computer power and telecommunications capability has been instrumental in facilitating this speed of change.

Marconi Plc, has, in the past, been one of the key driving forces of this change through its computing, avionics and telecommunications businesses, mainly within the UK and Europe.

However, over the past three years Marconi has decided to concentrate on developing its telecommunications business on a world-wide basis by organic product and organizational development and an aggressive programme of acquisition and divestment. The transformation of Marconi has successfully taken place in this comparatively short period of time and is being further accelerated by the unprecedented growth in the utilization of the Internet and World-Wide Web as a means of incredibly fast communication.

This new book provides some fascinating insights into how competition develops and changes across the whole value chain to the end consumer. It sets out clearly and comprehensively the variety of changes impacting on consumers and companies in a wide range of settings. The book provides a new and innovative way of considering the issues from both perspectives in a straightforward model that balances the various factors. Indeed, this may provide a framework for those responsible for developing regulations designed to ensure competitive markets and to protect consumer interests. The book's coverage of the issues is not only comprehensive, in that it includes aspects such as the role of regulation and environmental concerns, it is also authoritative and accessible.

I am delighted to see that David Asch and Brian Wolfe have included some of the latest thinking in the Marconi business, related to Global Supply Chain

Management. Brian has been part of the management team responsible for facilitating the rapid cultural change at Marconi and combined with David's academic background they have been able to present a thoughtful and balanced picture of this changing world. In some ways this partnership between an academic and a practising manager represents in a small way what we at Marconi seek to do by bringing together talent and ability from both public and private sectors for the benefit of all.

I am aware that the significant global changes in the way we do business have changed many aspects of the way in which business is conducted. This in turn has created new relationships, new competitive forces, new and often unforeseen and unforeseeable challenges, and new ways of working. The availability of this book will allow the consumer, student, and the academic and business community to better understand the new, changing and exciting times through which we are living.

George Simpson
CEO, Marconi PLC

29 August 2000

1 Introduction

Have you recently tried to buy anything in your local electrical goods supermarket? Well, we did, we wanted to buy a new fax machine. The prices were grouped as follows:

Type of fax machine	Retail price £
Thermal paper	100
Plain paper	150
Plain paper with e-mail facility	200

We had previously purchased a photocopying machine, only to find later that the cost of the replacement toner unit was as much as the cost of the original copier. So, we asked about the cost and availability of printer refills for the plain paper fax machine. No one in the store could tell us. We left the shop because we were not convinced that the shop assistant or the retailer itself really knew what they were selling, and we had no idea whether the price was competitive. We had lost confidence in this retailer's ability to offer a fair deal.

Are consumers really in a position to decide which product or service to buy and how much to pay for it? Are we all, as consumers, getting a fair deal? We will keep reverting to these questions of product or service and price. We make no apology for this. This is the core of what this book is all about. We will present a broad view of the argument by describing markets and their evolution and how they are supplied. Reference will also be made to government involvement through legislation and regulation.

How consumers make decisions about which item to buy and how much they pay, and the forces and factors that influence those decisions are some of the issues that this book seeks to address. The chain of activities that leads up to enabling them to make that choice, or not, is also an issue which is considered. Indeed, the central arguments that we seek to illuminate concern the wide range of information which bombards the consumer and buyer in addition to the simple benchmarks of price, availability, and quality. In order to do this, the nature of markets, and why some appear to be more competitive than others, is a key concern. Markets for goods and services do not exist in a vacuum, they are part and parcel of the communities and countries where they operate. As such, they are subject to overarching legal and regulatory frameworks which are designed to ensure that certain requirements are met in terms of health, safety and quality standards for some products, or whether or not a firm can control more than a certain percentage of the market.

Right at the outset we need to clarify our definition of markets. For us, and throughout the book, a market refers to the interaction of supply and demand. In other words it is the arena in which buyers and sellers come together for the purposes of exchange, and that may be a retail store, a commodity market, or a corporate buying office, to mention but three examples. Such markets are fundamental to the effective and efficient operation of a capitalist or market-based economy. They have been one of the key features in enabling living standards to rise in most advanced economies. Markets are generally assumed to balance supply and demand. The fact that supply and demand behaviours are different and opposite for buyers and sellers allows the system to find a price at which buyers will want to purchase exactly the amount that sellers want to sell, that is the equilibrium price. The equilibrium price depends on the relative power or strength of buyers and sellers. The establishment of an equilibrium price in effect allocates the goods to some buyers and withholds them from others; the market has also admitted some sellers to do business and denied that privilege to others. In this way the market is a means of excluding certain people from activity, namely customers with too little money or with too weak desires, or suppliers unwilling or unable to operate at a certain price. It is, in effect, a rationing mechanism (Heilbroner and Thurow, 1998).

The market system is efficient and dynamic, it is also devoid of values. It recognizes no valid claim to the goods and services of society except those of wealth and income. The blindness of the market to any claim on society's output except wealth or income creates very serious problems. This means that those who inherited large incomes are entitled to large shares of output, even though they have produced nothing themselves. It means that individuals who have no wealth and cannot produce have no way of gaining income through the economic mechanism. Consequently, every market society interferes to some extent with the outcome of the market system. It does so when an 'economic' problem crosses the line to become a 'social problem'. There are two other weaknesses in the market mechanism which we ought to discuss briefly at the outset.

First, the market system is built on the assumption that individuals are rational as well as acquisitive and that all buyers and sellers in the market will have at least roughly accurate information about the market. As we will discuss later (in Chapter 2) this is very often not the case for certain goods and services.

The second weakness has to do with the time horizon of market processes. Will markets provide a setting in which very long term, very risky, but potentially invaluable research and development take place? Consider for example the Internet. This was started some 25 years ago as a nuclear bomb-proof communications system. It has only recently become an arena where firms can make a lot of money. No private firm using normal decision-making rules would ever have made the original investment. The risks were too high, the time lags until profits could be made were too long. Using discounted net present values, that is, the usual mechanism for evaluating the value of future returns, today's market value of a pound or dollar that will not be received until ten years from now is approximately zero (Bowman and Asch, 1987). This would not have happened without social investments made with time horizons far beyond those of private firms. So investments in education, infrastructure, and research and development have to be at least partly financed by governments, as markets tend to under-provide them.

Markets can also be manipulated to the benefit of buyers or sellers. In Chapter 4 we discuss the role of the UK's Competition Commission in attempting to regulate the market in the UK.

There is only one way in which firms make profits on a sustained and sustainable basis, which is to add value for their customers and to do so in ways that other people cannot. Similarly, the fundamental uncertainties associated with the business will always come through, however sophisticated the financial engineering. Kay (1996) argues that the development of a vast array of complex financial instruments is unlikely to be of benefit unless they exploit distortions in the tax system. Changing the risk profile, and hence cost, of one part of the financial structure alters the risk pattern and cost of the rest. Business cannot be made better by creative financing.

Consider for a moment foreign trade (we look at globalization a little later in this chapter) which involves most firms of any size as but one example of the development of financial markets. In 1995 The Wall Street Journal estimated that transactions in foreign exchange markets were around $1.2 trillion a day – over 50 times the level of world trade. Around 95 per cent of these transactions are speculative in nature, often using complex new financial derivatives based on futures and options. Albert (1993, p.188) estimated that the daily volume of transactions on the world's foreign exchange markets totalled $900 bn which is equal to France's annual GDP. This virtual economy has the potential to disrupt the underlying real economy as the examples of the collapse of Barings Bank in 1995 and the Long Term

Capital Fund in 1998 demonstrated. Our concern is with the real economy of goods and services.

We will not be discussing the nature and role of the financial markets that have proliferated during the last decade and more. Indeed, it is possible to argue that many organizations become distracted by the needs of the financial markets to the detriment of their ability to manage their business and service the needs of their customers. In addition, an over-emphasis on a company's share price, and hence its value, often overlooks whether or not the firm is able to meet the needs of its customers now and in the future, and whether or not it is likely to be profitable in the medium to long term. In a similar way, we will not be emphasizing the role of mergers and acquisitions. Such activities lead to increasing levels of concentration on the supply side with little evidence that they provide benefits to the firms' customers, or indeed society as a whole. There have been exceptions to this generalization. GEC plc (now Marconi plc) has almost tripled its share price over the years 1998 to 2000, which was driven by a carefully considered corporate strategy aimed at moving the company into the highly profitable and growing telecommunications market.

In this chapter we will first address the main issues of concern to consumers and also to companies who seek to supply them. This will enable us to set out some of the main themes of the book, which concerns relationships between consumers in competitive markets, the role of regulation and whether or not a fair deal is being had by all. We will then look briefly at issues concerning the globalization of the economy. We conclude this introductory chapter by outlining and explaining the main structure of the book.

1.1 The Changing Nature of Competition

We will now look at three quite different examples of the changing nature of competition. They are drawn from three quite different industries or markets. They also provide an illustration of how we will use contemporary business issues to illuminate our understanding of the complex nature of markets and the ways in which buyers and sellers interact. First, consider Illustration 1.1 which looks at the launch of Windows 2000, the latest software development from Microsoft.

Illustration 1.1

Bill's Big Roll-Out

In some ways, the launch of Windows 2000 looks like a standard Microsoft event. Delivering bigger and supposedly better Windows operating systems every few years, to a carefully prepared and well-primed market, is what Microsoft does best.

But Windows 2000 is more than another upgrade. It is an entirely new operating system designed not only to take Microsoft, for the first time, into high-end computing – the big company datacentres where the hearts of companies reside – but also to give much-needed credibility to the firm's Internet and commerce strategy.

Microsoft's real goal is to achieve reliability and scalability (the ability to handle 'big iron' computers with up to 32 processors) comparable to that of high-end Unix systems, such as Sun Microsystems Solaris. In doing this, Microsoft is making a tacit admission that the market has turned against small servers that multiply like rabbits across corporate networks and lead to spiralling administrative costs.

Server consolidation and a return to centralised control over networks are also being driven by the demands of Internet computing and e-business. As companies use the Internet to get deep into the systems of their suppliers and reach out to their business customers, they can no longer predict the number of potential users they will have on their network. Operating systems that do not scale up just cannot cut it.

E-commerce also puts huge demands on the reliability of computer systems. If departmental applications crash, or if the servers they run on need re-booting every few days, it may be a cause for grumbling, but it won't put you out of business. However, the moment you start transferring a large part of your activities to the web, system failures, however brief, can be disastrous.

So vital has it been for Microsoft to achieve 'five nines' reliability (99.999 per cent up-time), which even smaller firms doing business on the web now demand, that it has deliberately sacrificed what used to be the *sine qua non* of Windows operating systems – something called 'backwards applications compatibility'. Previous versions of Windows could at least be relied on to run even the most ancient software.

Despite its troubled and extended gestation, demand for the new product is high. Not only will it replace all the NT systems that are currently running, but also it will slowly start to eat into parts of the fragmented Unix market.

Even though few Unix shops expect to defect now, the combination of Microsoft's volume pricing model and the 'withering' of the Unix skills base will ensure the success of Windows 2000. Despite the renewed efforts of Hewlett-Packard and IBM in the Unix market, only Sun appears to have the momentum and support to see off the threat. The wild card is Linux, the fast-growing (and free) Unix-based operating system. Linux is taking about 17 per cent of the server market and growing at the expense of both NT and other Unix systems. It may lack the features of Windows 2000, but because its source code is open it can be easily fixed or modified. And free is free.

Not all the elements of Microsoft's strategy appear as solid as the prospects for Windows 2000. The consumer versions of Windows that will succeed Windows 98 will have to be easier to use and cheaper than today's product. Hardware components and the prices of consumer PCs are tumbling so fast that the $40 per copy that Microsoft is thought to charge its best industry customers is increasingly hard to justify. The still-intimidating complexity of the PC, a failing to which Microsoft readily admits, contrasts unfavourably with the new generation of Internet-ready games consoles, such as Sony's PlayStation 2, which will be launched next year.

Nor is it clear that Microsoft will be more than a bit-player in the exploding market for Internet access and information devices. Its Windows CE operating system is fine in podgy sub-notebook computers, but it has been trounced by the Palm operating system in the market for smaller devices. Meanwhile, the Symbian joint venture between Psion, Nokia, Ericsson, Matsushita and Motorola seems likely to provide the dominant operating system for smart mobile phones.

As for the billions that Microsoft is pouring into cable and telecoms, that could turn out to be either an inspired move or a fruitless attempt to buy influence. Has this investment had any effect on the pace at which consumer broadband services are rolled out? Even if Windows CE gets into more set-top boxes, companies such as AT&T have no intention of falling into a dependency relationship on Microsoft like that of PC makers. By working with partners on pilot services, Microsoft is 'accelerating its learning.'

And even though Microsoft appears to be embracing the notion of applications hosting on the web, this is a model that spells danger. Such software may well be offered free by rivals, such as Sun with its new personal productivity suite, with the money being made up on services – an area where Microsoft is weak. The threat to Office may be distant, but it is real.

The broader question for Microsoft is whether being the most accomplished fast follower the world has seen is any longer an advantage, given the speed with which innovative ideas can be brought to market on the Internet. The reorganisation earlier this year has pulled Microsoft closer to its customers and reinvigorated its best managers by giving them more autonomy. It is, however, a 30,000-strong company with bureaucratic habits and a penchant for fixing problems by throwing blood and money at them. That may have worked for Windows 2000, but it won't always.

Source: The Economist, 18 September 1999

As well as discussing the nature of the challenges facing Microsoft, the article identifies that Microsoft's new products, that is software, need to demonstrate considerable improvements on existing software suites. Various changes to the software are discussed, for example reliability and scalability, and the need for the changes identified. These changes include the externally driven changes to the software market concerning the development of e-commerce and a return to centralized control over corporate computer networks.

If some of the changes to the product, such as scalability and reliability referred to above, are positive changes then it is interesting to observe that in order to achieve this, Microsoft has had to sacrifice backwards applications compatibility. Their assessment of the changing needs in a rapidly developing marketplace meant that in this case this was a sacrifice worth making. The positive note for Microsoft in the article refers to the withering of the skills base to sustain alternative operating systems such as Unix. But, Sun is still a major competitor and the free Unix based operating system called Linux and the impact it may have is still a largely unknown quantity. For corporate customers then there are a number of alternatives to Windows 2000, but as the article concludes, it is still likely to be successful.

Consumer versions of the new Windows 2000 products need to be easier to use and cheaper than the current version. However, individual consumers are likely to have less choice as to the form of the operating systems when they acquire a PC. Nevertheless, as the article notes, Microsoft faces some very competent competitors in a market in which it is a bit player. Sony's new PlayStation will be Internet-ready and considerably easier to use than a PC. The growing market for Internet access and information devices is likely to be dominated by non-Microsoft products. Also the large firms involved in cable and telecoms are unlikely again to develop a dependency relationship with Microsoft in the same way that PC makers did. So although the short and medium term outlook for Microsoft appears to be reasonably positive, the medium to long term is likely to pose considerable problems. It is possible to see that existing competitors in their different markets (for example, Sun and Sony), are likely to pose significant challenges to Microsoft's position. Furthermore, it is also likely that Microsoft's dominance in PC software will be challenged by firms that do not yet exist in what is after all one of the world's fastest changing industries. All this is likely to mean that customers, whether corporate or individual, are likely to have a wider choice of better software products in the future.

We will now turn our attention to a completely different industry. Illustration 1.2 looks at the market for functional foods. The article describes the nature of the market and some interesting paradoxes that confront firms in the industry.

Illustration 1.2

Functional Foods

Whether you call 'functional foods' 'nutraceuticals' or 'designer foods', they sound just as unappetising. Yet this value-added grub, which promises health benefits beyond what the nutrients would normally provide, is touted as the panacea not only for drug firms looking to exploit their science, but also for food companies struggling to boost their profits.

The distinction between food and drugs is increasingly blurred. Firms in America and Europe now sell margarines containing plant biochemicals called stanols to lower blood cholesterol, or tomato ketchup packed with lycopenes to protect against cancer. Firms in Japan, Australia and Europe have long supplied yogurt and fermented drinks full of probiotic bacteria that claim to boost immunity and improve digestion.

The market for functional foods is currently worth $17bn in America, $10bn in Japan and $14bn in Europe, according to Nutrition Business Journal. That is only 3 per cent of the $1.5 trillion-a-year global food industry. However, with food companies' sales growing little faster than inflation, the 25 per cent-a-year growth in demand for functional foods is irresistible.

Functional foods command premium prices. A tub of Benecol sells for £2.49 ($3.99) in Britain, compared with less than £1 for normal margarine. Nestlé's LC-1 bacteria-enhanced yogurt commands a 40 per cent price premium over the conventional stuff.

As consumers grow richer, older and better educated they are becoming more health-conscious. In a survey of 1000 Americans by the International Food Information Council, two-thirds of those ready to buy food for their health were over 45 years old. More than 60 per cent had gone to college and earned at least $50,000 a year. This is theoretically a perfect market for food companies. But companies are struggling to identify customers. Health-conscious consumers already eat healthily and do not need specialised foods. The poor, who suffer most from heart disease, cannot afford functional foods.

In Nestlé's head office in Vevey, Peter Brabeck-Letmathe, the chief executive, proudly shows off a table full of new supercharged foods: 'Our nutritional division is a major, major growth driver for the future. It transforms commodities vulnerable to private-label competition into high-priced premium products.' The FDA may soon endorse the claim that soya protein can reduce the risk of heart disease. This could lead to a new class of products from companies including Monsanto, a life-sciences firm, and Con Agra and Archer Daniels Midland, two agricultural giants.

Yet functional food has so far been a flop. Campbell Soup dropped its Intelligent Quinine frozen food after last year's disappointing consumer trials, despite having spent more than $50m on it. Kellogg this summer halted the American launch of its Ensemble brand, saying it wanted to improve its marketing. And in January Denmark's MD Foods stopped the British sale of its Pact products after disputes over their supposed benefits.

A critical report from the Centre for Science in the Public Interest (CSPI) asserts that these superfoods have not, at least so far, fulfilled their promises. In Europe and America too, consumers have become increasingly suspicious of exaggerated, often contradictory health claims.

The labyrinthine regulation of functional foods is partly to blame. Japanese firms do not need regulatory approval, provided they do not claim to treat or prevent a disease. But they can still make assertions about health, many of which are dubious. Of Japan's 1,100 functional foods, only 15 per cent have official approval. Consumers waste trillions of yen on products purporting to cure every known ailment from bad breath to stress.

America follows a similar logic. Anyone can make a claim about structure or function – that cranberry juice, say, helps urinary-tract health. But for a label to assert that it 'prevents urinary-tract infection', a disease, requires the approval of the FDA. Only a handful of firms have bothered, among them Quaker Oats for soluble oat fibre and Kellogg for psyllium husk.

Not surprisingly, these fine distinctions are lost on the public. And in the United States, advertisements are not regulated by the FDA, so they make health claims that labels cannot. No wonder consumers are confused.

Functional foods have, by and large, been poorly branded. Instead of selling a way of life, as with other consumer products, advertisements for functional foods are laced with technical jargon about how the product works, ignoring such things as taste. Functional foods have none of the coherence or emotional appeal of organic or vegetarian foods.

Distribution is also tricky. Novartis plans to sell Aviva in separate areas of supermarkets. By contrast, Yakult has had huge success distributing small bottles of fermented milk alongside normal dairy products. Others think pharmacies or health-food shops are the way to go. One of the reasons why Nestlé would like to gain full control of L'Oréal, the French cosmetics giant in which it holds a large indirect stake, is the chance of creating a new distribution channel.

Drug firms have the scientific expertise, wealth and experience to satisfy health regulators; food companies understand brands and consumers. Both are needed for functional foods to become a mass product. Even then dubious claims for some functional foods could ruin prospects for the rest.

Source: The Economist, 11 September 1999

Illustration 1.2 is a fine example of how the boundaries of a particular market, in this case functional foods, is really quite indeterminate. Are the products of the firms which operate in this industry food or drugs? An interesting paradox that this case demonstrates concerns the nature of the market for these particular foodstuffs. The article notes that these products command a significant price premium over equivalent conventional products, largely because the market into which they are selling consists of older, wealthier individuals. Unfortunately for the producers, identifying customers can be a problem since the wealthy health-conscious consumers already eat healthily so their requirement for specialized foods with such additives is reduced. The poorer sections of the population are unlikely to be able to afford this particular group of products.

In addition to confusion over the boundaries of the market, that is, are these food products or are they drugs?, the case provides a good example of how the regulatory framework influences the marketplace. Clearly few would dissent from the need for organizations such as the FDA to control drugs so that they provide a safe treatment regime for particular ailments. However, the case demonstrates that consumers can be confused, that is their knowledge of the market and their understanding of what the particular product provides may be less than perfect, due to legalistic manoeuvres by sellers which effectively appear to subvert the control and protection provided by a regulatory framework. This example also demonstrates the difficulty that some producers may have in accessing a big enough market for their products, that is, do they have access to an appropriate distribution network? This is an issue to which we will return later, in Chapter 3. Finally, it is always open to producers who are unable to sell sufficient quantities of their product to move the product into a different part of the market. Producers could make their products more readily available to other sections of the population by reducing prices, for example. They face a trade-off between selling fewer items at a higher price and selling more at a lower price. Conventional cost-volume-profit analysis would help address the issues involved in making such a move in this example.

Our last example in this chapter considers the changes made in the entertainment industry. Illustration 1.3 focuses on the proposed media merger between Viacom and CBS. Unlike our previous two examples this case also brings out explicitly the way in which the personalities of those running major organizations are likely to affect their future development. Although we will not focus on the human side of the organization in this book it is as well to keep it in mind when considering the decisions that organizations make. As the article demonstrates, there are a number of large global companies where the personality of the chief executive is an important dimension in the way in which the firm makes decisions and conducts its business.

Illustration 1.3

Two Sharks in a Fishbowl

On September 7 Viacom, one of America's largest entertainment companies, announced that it was planning to buy CBS, a broadcasting network, for $36bn. The deal, the largest-ever media merger, was welcomed as a stroke of strategic brilliance. Both companies' share prices leapt.

If this has not induced a sense of *déjà vu* on Wall Street, it should have. On 31 July 1995, Disney, one of America's biggest entertainment companies, announced that it was buying Capital Cities/ABC, a broadcasting network, for $19bn. The deal, the largest ever media merger, was welcomed as a stroke of strategic brilliance. Both companies' share prices leapt.

Four years later, the view of Disney's deal has changed. Disney's share price has plunged this year, and its chief executive, Michael Eisner, has spent a hot summer being grilled by an unfavourable press. Top of most of the lists of complaints is the weakness of ABC.

The network is seen as having done little for Disney. It has not yet turned any Disney show into a hit, and has not, according to Disney executives, done enough to promote the one big Disney show that it airs, Sunday night's 'The Wonderful World of Disney', presented by Mr Eisner. It trails NBC and CBS in the ratings, and Robert Iger, the network's chairman, describes its financial performance as 'disappointing'.

But then, neither has Disney done much for ABC. Its announcement in July that ABC was to merge with Disney's television-production operations caused an internal revolt. Besides the huge cultural and geographical problem of moving a New York-based business to Los Angeles, there have been some pretty big ego problems – which resulted in the resignation, last month, of its programming chief, Jamie Tarses.

Yet, say the many defenders of the Viacom-CBS merger, these are flaws of implementation. The strategic thinking behind both mergers is impeccable.

And that is true. The merger of Viacom and CBS is part of a five-year-long restructuring of the industry, involving all the world's big media companies. They are turning into outfits that produce content and distribute it through as many channels as possible (see Table below). So 'Rugrats' started life as a cartoon on its Nickelodeon cable channel, has been turned into a film (made by Paramount, Viacom's Hollywood studio), a book (published by Simon & Schuster, Viacom's publisher) and a website, and has been sold on chocolates, pyjamas and God-knows-what through Viacom's merchandising arm. These revenue streams make money and also promote the 'Rugrats' brand.

If the new firm works this way - as Sumner Redstone, Viacom's boss, who will head it, and Mel Karmazin, CBS's chief, both hope – the network will get a boost from a future 'Rugrats', and *vice versa*. Broadcasting networks remain the best way to reach a huge audience, yet with ratings sliding and costs rising, they make sense only if they are used as a shop window for programmes that are sold profitably into syndication.

On the advertising side, too, the merger looks a fine idea. Viacom-CBS will command around $5.5bn in national television-advertising revenues, more than any other company in the world. Viacom's young audience (for networks such as MTV and Nickelodeon) complements CBS's oldish one. And CBS brings with it extensive radio and billboard businesses. No media company's advertising salesmen will be able to offer their customers a wider choice.

Putting the pieces together

	Time Warner	Disney	Viacom-CBS	Sony	Bertels-mann	News Corpn	Seagram
Revenues, $bn	26.8	23.0	18.9	17.5	14.4	12.8	10.4
TV production	/	/	/	/	/	/	/
Film production	/	/	/	/	/	/	/
Music	/	/		/	/		/
Publishing	/	/	/		/	/	
Radio		/	/		/		
Broadcast TV	/	/	/			/	
Cable TV	/	/	/	/		/	/
Satellite TV				/	/	/	
Internet	/	/	/	/	/	/	/
Theme parks	/	/					/
Shops	/	/	/		/		/

What is more, advertising revenue has boomed in recent years. Some think that is just volatility; others reckon that there has been a fundamental change in advertising's favour. 'Because the product cycle has shortened, advertising spending has been rising faster than GDP,' says Chris Dixon, of Paine-Webber. 'This company will be in a great position to take advantage of that.'

Lights, camera, implementation

As, presumably, should Disney-ABC be, but for the difficulty of making the thing work. Unfortunately, implementation is not a secondary issue – and implementing mergers in the media business is harder than it is in most other industries.

If the merger is allowed to go ahead, Mr Redstone and Mr Karmazin will have to work out how to make the broadcast and production assets work together. If they try to merge their operations, they will face similar difficulties to Disney's. If they do not, and CBS is allowed to behave as though it were independent, the merger will look pointless.

But the biggest obstacle is likely to be Mr Redstone and Mr Karmazin themselves. 'Two sharks in a fishbowl' is how the boss of a rival describes them. The ego problem is not exclusive to the media business, but it seems to loom larger. That may be because show-business attracts showy types; or because some big media companies are run by founder-managers, such as Mr Redstone and Rupert Murdoch, who created their empires by the force of their own personalities and show no sign of mellowing with old age.

Mr Redstone seems to have got tougher and more ambitious with age. He spent most of his working life putting together a chain of movie theatres, but it was with the purchase of Viacom, a cable company, when he was 63, that his career took off. Seven years later, he bought Paramount, a movie studio. As a boss, he is inexhaustible, and exhausting. He has already fired two anointed successors and the latest has now been shoved aside in favour of the 55-year-old Mr Karmazin.

If Mr Redstone is not the ideal boss, neither is Mr Karmazin the perfect subordinate. He did a good job getting CBS into shape. He also managed to get rid of Michael Jordan, the chief executive who had made him chief operating officer, and took his job. Mr Redstone will never go easily; but he will find Mr Karmazin almost impossible to unseat. According to his contract, he can be fired only with the agreement of 14 members of the 18-member board – of which eight will come from CBS.

In theory, the fit is as neat as the strategists say. The reality, unless Mr Redstone goes, risks being a nasty mess.

Source: The Economist, 11 September 1999

This case is of particular interest because of the insight it gives us into the changing nature of industries and markets. Who would have thought a mere decade or so ago that there would be strong connections, synergies even, between, for example, book publishing and film and TV production? While the processes, at a superficial level at least, between making programmes for

TV, cable TV, satellite TV, and films for cinemas is fairly obvious, the connection with shops and book publishing is perhaps less so. The way in which firms in the industry have been able to maximize their returns on the investment in content (for example, in 'Rugrats'), is a good example of the power of the distribution chain. The firms concerned have been able to generate a return by effectively cross-selling related items such as books and clothing, based on the original concept. It also demonstrates that the way in which the industry is developing means that the development of a particular product, for example a film destined for release through the cinema, may be heavily dependent on its potential for subsequent video sales, cable and satellite TV, and cross-selling into books, clothing, and music. The other point demonstrated in this example is the power of the merged groups to command large sums of advertising revenue. In an almost classic sense it also demonstrates the determination of the companies concerned to span all levels of the market from young audiences to older ones.

It is also interesting to consider briefly the antecedents of some of the companies identified in the article. News Corporation started life as an Australian publisher of newspapers before branching out into other parts of the media world. Sony on the other hand is perhaps best known as one of the world's finest producers of electrical equipment such as hi-fi's, video cameras, the ubiquitous 'walkman', and so on that later bought its way into the media and entertainment industry. Interestingly we mentioned the Sony Playstation as a potential competitor for Microsoft earlier in this chapter. As the article itself notes, Disney is an amalgamation of TV and film production with broadcast TV. As these very different organizations continue to develop in a broadly defined entertainment industry, we are likely to witness increasing levels of concentration of ownership. The resultant control over substantial and significant media interests may not always be in the public interest.

If we now take a moment to think about the issues raised in the three examples that we have just reviewed we can see that there are a number of common themes. Sellers and producers have been driven to sell increasing volumes of goods and services. Some were focusing on a higher value added sector (for example functional foods) while others were beginning to come under some considerable pressure on pricing (for example Microsoft). We have been able to observe that different firms have chosen to compete in different ways. So Microsoft has one approach to the server market while Sun has another. Similarly, the way in which Sony approaches the market for Internet devices is quite different to Microsoft, just as in the same way its approach to the media industry has been quite different to Disney's. However, all the industries that we have looked appear to be subjected to increasing levels of concentration. This may reduce levels of competition, and hence consumer choice, and most countries or regions, for example the US, EU, or the UK have regulatory frameworks designed to ensure that competition is allowed to flourish. We will consider this in more detail in Chapter 4.

Potentially the most interesting feature of these examples concerns the changing nature of industries and markets. For example, would we have predicted Microsoft's dominance in the PC market in the early 1980s? Perhaps by 2003 Microsoft may not be a dominant player at all? Could we have conceived a mere 20 years ago that Sony might compete with Microsoft on the one hand, with Disney on the other, let alone Matsushita for electrical goods? The lesson surely is that one of the most difficult tasks is to predict the nature, scale and scope of changes at an industry level. The dynamism of the market system referred to earlier provides the impetus for product evolution and development and uncertainty for those already in the game as to the likely future direction of their particular arena. For us, this is what makes it so exciting.

1.2 Globalization

Globalization is a phenomenon that affects us wherever we may be. There are a number of reasons for the growing influence of globalization. The technology of communication whereby we can talk to colleagues, arrange financing, buy and sell shares almost anywhere in the world by phone and computer screen is a large part of the answer. Technology developments in transportation are also a key development in the globalization of the world economy. In many ways we seem to be operating in a truly global market. Think for moment of the labels that you see on the produce in your local supermarket or grocery store. Much of the produce comes from areas outside the home country in a way that had not been conceived off a relatively short time ago. Table 1.1 illustrates how dependent the European economies are on world trade. For the 15 EU countries 51 per cent of the Gross Domestic product (GDP) relate to imports and exports of goods and services. It is notable that the US (21 per cent) and Japan (18 per cent) have far lower percentages; nevertheless the proportion of GDP that world trade represents is still very significant.

For consumers this is a very good development on the surface. But globalization raises two issues for producers. One is that goods made at home often have to compete with goods made in countries that do not impose UK or EU standards on their own producers, such as not using sweat shop or child labour, observing a 40 hour week, and so on. Is this 'fair competition' for those Europeans who are trying to produce these goods at home? Secondly, if foreign goods displace EU ones because they are cheaper, what happens to

Table 1.1	*Imports and exports as a percentage of GDP in 1998*		
France	44	United Kingdom	43
Germany	46	EU 15	51
Italy	39	Japan	18
Spain	41	USA	21

Sources: Eurostatistics, 8–9, 1999; UN Monthly Bulletin of Statistics, July 1999

EU workers who lose their jobs? Part of the process of globalization is that wages are driven down in higher wage countries and gradually increased in lower wage ones. Or it produces unemployment because European manufacturers are forced to automate processes to reduce the number of relatively highly paid staff. The same is true of returns on capital. So globalization tends to be a leveller. Globalization changes our world because it increases economic competitiveness and political defensiveness.

Multinational companies whose business empires straddle the globe are also a principal driver behind globalization. Companies such as Coca-Cola, Ford, IBM, Phillips, BP-Amoco, McKinsey and so on, operate all round the world. So if you buy a Coca-Cola in France you are buying a US product that was manufactured in that country. The movement toward the internationalization of production is a phenomenon that embraces the US, Europe and Japan. The organization and management of the supply chain has become a key issue for firms which we discuss in Chapter 5. Some time ago the United Nations surveyed the size of the world of the multinationals. It was noted that the 350 largest multinationals had a combined turnover of $2700 bn in 1985. That was 30 per cent of the entire GNP of the world market economy and larger by several hundreds of billions of dollars than the combined GNP of all the pre-industrial economies, China included (Piel 1992).

We should not think of multinationals only as foreign enterprises seeking to invade someone else's market. They also include enterprises that have located branches abroad to invade their own home markets. The real challenge in the multinational is their ability to move technology around the world and innovate as they do so. How does a country hold on to a technological edge if its own companies are transferring that technology to foreign sites? More and more of the large companies of the world have come to consider their natural markets to be the globe, not just their home country. The struggle in cars, in computers, in telecommunications is for shares of a world market. Such companies then consider the global arena as their oyster, not only with regard to the sourcing of raw materials but to the location of plants and the direction of sales effort. With modern organization, systems of production, distribution, and communication the manufacture of commodities is more and more easily moved to whichever countries produce them most cheaply, whereas their sale is forced on the countries that represent the richest markets. So we might have a transistor radio whose parts are made in Hong Kong, China, or South Korea, which is assembled in Portugal and sold in the UK by a Japanese manufacturer. But these multinationals will only stay ahead if they innovate. Failure to do so will mean that competition will overtake them in the race for achieving a global 'trading edge'.

This can have interesting effects. Should a country wish to slow down its economy through monetary policy such as higher interest rates designed to reduce plant and equipment spending, restricted monetary policy at home may be nullified by the ability of a multinational to borrow abroad in order to finance its investment at home. Conversely, a monetary policy designed to stimulate the home economy may end up in loans that increase production in someone else's economy. Stimulatory fiscal policies may increase the demand for goods and services but that demand may focus on imported product rather than product produced locally. So the effectiveness of national economic policymaking weakens.

The desire of nation states to retain control over productive activity within their own borders runs up against the powerful counter-thrust of transnational corporations looking for markets without much regard to national boundaries. The multinational is in a position to win hard bargains from the host country that it seeks to enter if the corporation possesses new technologies and management techniques that the host nation seeks. Once a multinational has entered a foreign nation it becomes a hostage of the host country. It is now bound by the laws of the country and may find itself obliged to undertake policies different from those of its home country. At the same time the nation of which it is now hostage itself becomes hostage to the forces of global competition often with disconcerting results. Take the problem of a multinational that is forced by falling demand to cut back the volume of output. The decision on strictly economic lines would lead to closure of its least profitable plant. This may bring very serious economic repercussions in the particular nation in which the plant is located – so serious that the government will threaten to take action if the plant closes. What dictates shall the multinational then follow – those of standard business accounting or those of political accounting?

The sovereignty issue arises in acute form in regional trading blocks such as the European Union or North American Free Trade Association. If such groups are to be successful they must harmonize rules and regulations to enable firms to compete on a level playing field where the regulations they face are the same from country to country. If such harmonization did not occur firms would simply move to the country with the fewest rules and regulations. Yet each harmonization limits the power of national governments to change the same rules and regulations.

Some commentators are critical of increasing economic globalization. 'There is nothing in today's global market that buffers it against the strains arising from highly uneven economic development within and between the world's diverse societies. The swift waxing and waning of industries and livelihoods, the sudden shifts of production and capital, the casino of currency speculation – these conditions trigger counter-movements that challenge the very ground rules of the global free market.' (Gray 1998, p.7.)

Globalization is a phenomenon that is going to become of increasing importance in the future. Here we have only touched on and hinted at some of the complex issues involved. Our purpose has been merely to introduce globalization as an issue that we all have to consider because it affects us in day-to-day activities whether we like it or not. Whole books have been written about developments in the global economy or about the effects of globalization and so on. All we have tried to do is to introduce briefly some of the important effects as these will serve to inform the discussions that we have later in the book.

1.3 Outline of the Book

The book continues to develop the themes that we have identified in this introductory chapter. Chapter 2 considers the way we as consumers behave. We look at perceptions of price, value and quality as well as considering the decision processes that buyers go through in making a decision. The chapter concludes by considering a sophisticated framework for understanding consumers. The focus then shifts in Chapter 3 to develop an understanding of how markets work. We concentrate here on how industries and markets develop and on understanding the way in which competition appears to work. These two chapters together provide the backdrop to Chapter 4 where we consider the legislative and regulatory framework that exists in the EU and other areas of the world. The chapter also addresses whether or not consumers are over-protected and looks forward to the developing concerns around the environment and health and safety. Chapter 5 shifts the focus to considering supply chain management. Here we emphasize the need to ensure that managing the supply chain fits the firm's corporate strategy and discuss examples from some of the best organizations around the world. Chapter 6 then marks the first stage of bringing these themes together. We do this by looking at five different markets – personal computers, international air travel, telecommunications, cars, and retailing. The final chapter in the book looks to the future and marks the second stage of bringing the themes together. The focus here is on considering developments in information and communications technologies and the effect that these will have on the way we acquire goods and services. We note that all involved will need to change their paradigm as most of the historic 'rules of the game' will not be applicable. The implications for the legislative and regulatory framework are also considered, as are comparative levels of investment in ICTs, for example between the US and Europe.

2 Consumer Views

Consumer behaviour is a very complex matter. Indeed whole books have been written on the subject and it is not our intention here to go to that level of detail. What we will endeavour to do is to introduce some of the key ideas that inform us as to how consumers approach the complex process of buying goods and services. The chapter starts by introducing some basic elements of consumer behaviour including cultural, social, personal, and psychological factors. We consider how consumers perceive price and value and go on to examine consumers' perceptions of quality. We also draw out some of the implications for producers. A way of understanding differences between goods and services is then explored. While recognizing that one simple model cannot capture all elements of consumers' decision processes, we use a simple five-stage framework to identify the key issues. We conclude the chapter by developing a comprehensive model for understanding the issues which influence not only how consumers behave, but also how suppliers may respond.

2.1 Consumer Behaviour

Our decisions as consumers are not made in a vacuum. Consumer purchases are highly influenced by a range of factors including the cultural, social, personal, and psychological. We will consider briefly each of these in turn.

Cultural factors

Cultural factors probably have the broadest and deepest influence on consumer behaviour. Culture is the most fundamental determinant of a person's wants and behaviour. The child growing up in society learns a basic set of values, perceptions, preferences, and behaviour through a process of socialization involving the family and other key institutions. In addition, each culture contains smaller groups of subcultures that provide more specific identification and socialization for its members. Nationality groups are often found within large communities and exhibit distinct ethnic tastes and proclivities. Religious groups represent subcultures with specific cultural preferences and taboos. Racial groups may have distinct cultural styles and attitudes, while geographic areas often develop distinct subcultures with characteristic lifestyles.

Virtually all societies exhibit social stratification. Stratification sometimes takes the form of a caste system where the members of different castes are reared for certain roles and cannot change their caste membership. More frequently, stratification takes the form of social classes. Social classes are relatively homogeneous and enduring divisions in society, which are hierarchically ordered, and whose members share similar values, interest, and behaviour. Social classes have several characteristics. First, people within each social class tend to behave more alike than persons from different social classes. Second, persons are perceived as occupying inferior or superior positions according to their social class. Third, a person's social class is indicated by a number of variables such as income, wealth, education, and value orientation, rather than by any single variable. Fourth, individuals are able to move from one social class to another during their lifetime. The extent of this mobility varies according to the rigidity of social stratification in a given society. As one would expect, social classes show distinct product and brand preferences in terms of the products and services that they buy. They also differ in their media preferences as well as having language differences.

Social factors

Social factors such as reference groups, family, social roles and statuses also influence our behaviour as consumers. A person's reference groups are those groups that could have a direct or indirect influence on their attitudes or behaviour. Groups having a direct influence on an individual are membership groups. These are groups to which the person belongs and interacts. Some are primary groups with which there is a fairly continuous interaction, such as family, friends, neighbours and co-workers. Such groups tend to be informal. The person also belongs to secondary groups, which tend to be more formal and where there is less continuous interaction. Secondary groups might include religious organizations, professional associations and trade unions. Groups in which they are not members also influence people. Groups to which a person would like to belong are called aspirational groups. The importance of reference group influence varies amongst products and brands.

Members of the buyer's family can exercise a strong influence on behaviour. The family of orientation consists of one's parents, from whom we acquire an orientation towards religion, politics, economics, and a sense of personal ambition, self worth, and so on. Even if the buyer no longer interacts very much with his or her parents, their influence on the unconscious behaviour of the buyer can be significant. In countries where parents continue to live with their children, the influence can be substantial. A more direct influence on everyday buying behaviour is one's immediate family, normally one's spouse or partner and children.

People participate in many groups throughout life — family, clubs, and organizations. The person's position in each group can be defined in terms of role and status. Each role carries a status reflecting the general esteem accorded to it by society. Products are often used to communicate an individual's role and status in society. Many products have the potential to become status symbols. However, status symbols vary for different social classes and also geographically.

Personal factors

A buyer's decisions are also influenced by their personal characteristics, especially their age and life-cycle stage, occupation, economic circumstances, lifestyle, and personality. Most people change the goods and services they buy over their lifetime. People's taste in clothes, furniture, and recreation is also age-related. Consumption may also be shaped by the stage of the family life cycle. Target markets are often defined as certain life-cycle groups for which appropriate products and services have been designed. A person's consumption pattern is also influenced by their occupation. Certain occupational groups have above-average interest in particular products and services; indeed a company may specialize in producing products needed by a particular occupational group. An individual's economic circumstances will greatly affect product choice. Their economic circumstances consist of their disposable income (its level, stability, and timing), savings and assets, borrowing power, and attitude towards spending as opposed to saving.

People coming from the same subculture, social class, and even occupation may lead quite different lifestyles. An individual's lifestyle is their pattern of living in the world as expressed in their activities, interest and opinions. As such, lifestyle betrays the individual interacting with the environment, and reflects something beyond their social class on the one hand or personality on the other. If we know someone's social class, we can infer several things about their likely behaviour but fail to see them as an individual. If we know someone's personality we may be able to infer distinguishing psychological characteristics but not much about actual activities, interests and opinions. Lifestyle attempts to profile a whole person's pattern of acting in the world.

Each person has a distinct personality that will influence their buying behaviour. An individual's personality is usually described in terms of such traits as self-confidence, dominance, autonomy, deference, sociability, defensiveness, and adaptability.

Psychological factors

Our buying choices are also influenced by number of psychological factors such as motivation, perception, learning, and beliefs and attitudes. At any given time individuals may have many needs. Some may arise from physiological causes such as the need for food and basic necessities. Others may arise from psychological causes such as the need for recognition, esteem, or belonging. Most of these needs will not be intense enough to motivate the person to act at a particular point in time. A need becomes a motive when it is aroused to a sufficient level of intensity. The motivated person is ready to act. How they act is influenced by their perception of the situation. Two people in the same motivated state and objective situation may act quite differently because they perceive the situation differently. Perception is the process by which an individual selects, organizes, and interprets information inputs to create a meaningful picture of the world. As such it depends not only on the nature of the physical stimuli, but also on the relation of the stimuli to the surrounding field and on conditions within the individual. Selective exposure, selected distortion, and selective retention influence our perception of an object or event. We are exposed to an enormous number of stimuli every day. It is impossible for us to attend to all of the stimuli – most will be screened out. So the real challenge for a firm is to identify which stimuli people will notice. Even stimuli that we notice do not necessarily come across in the intended way. Each of us attempts to fit incoming information into our existing mindset. Selected distortion describes the tendency of people to twist information into personal meanings. We also tend to interpret information in a way that will support rather than challenge our preconceptions. People will forget much of what they learn. They tend to retain information that supports their attitudes and beliefs.

Learning describes changes in an individual's behaviour arising from experience – most human behaviour is learned. An individual's learning is produced through a complex interplay of drives, stimuli, cues, responses and reinforcement. A drive is a strong internal stimulus impelling action and becomes a motive when it is directed toward a particular drive-reducing stimulus object. Seeing advertisements, articles, hearing about special offers are all cues that can influence our response. If the experience with the good or service is rewarding then our response to that particular item will be reinforced. We acquire our beliefs and attitudes through acting and learning;

these in turn influence our buying behaviour. Beliefs are descriptive thoughts that we hold about something; they may be based on knowledge, opinion, or faith. An attitude describes a person's enduring favourable or unfavourable cognitive evaluations, emotional feelings, and tendencies towards some object or idea. We have attitudes to almost everything. Attitudes lead us to behave in fairly consistent ways towards similar objects. As such we do not have to interpret and react to every object in a fresh way because attitudes economize on energy and thought. Attitudes are thus very difficult to change.

We have just outlined, briefly, the many forces that affect consumer behaviour. A consumer's choice is the result of a complex interplay of cultural, social, personal, and psychological factors. Although firms may not be able to influence many of these factors, they are useful in identifying buyers that might have the most interest in a particular product or service. Other factors may be subject to influence by the firm who can then develop appropriate marketing information to attract a strong consumer response.

2.2 Consumers' Perception of Price and Value

We can define value as the perceived worth of benefits received by a customer in exchange for the price paid for a product offering. It is what the customer 'gets' in relation to what they 'give'. Buyers frequently form frames of reference when making buying decisions. These frames of reference influence how they respond to price and product information (Smith and Nagle, 1995). These authors argue that framing, which is grounded in prospect theory (which integrates the psychology of decision evaluations with the economic theory of consumer choice), challenges the economic idea that people compare the positive utility of having a good with the negative utility of its price. Instead, they argue that people evaluate purchases in terms of gains or losses relative to a reference point. This has three implications. First, transactions can be structured to reflect gains and avoid perceived losses. Second, decision outcomes can be specifically described as gains or losses. Third, gains or losses can be combined as bundles that increase the perceived value of the combination.

Structuring transactions to reflect gains and avoid losses

One implication is to frame the actual price relative to a higher reference price, as discounts from a higher price rather than as premiums over a lower price. For example, hotels normally state their room rates as the highest they charge during peak demand periods and discount those rates most of the time. If the explicit base price was seen as the starting point, buyers paying a higher price will view their failure to qualify for discounts as gain-denied. They will find that less objectionable than being charged a premium, which they would view as an explicit loss. Because losses loom larger than gains, it is more painful to consumers to give up an asset then it is pleasurable to obtain it. So, buyers are biased in favour of retaining the *status quo*, of keeping the assets that they already own. Consequently, it is often better to decouple product acquisition and payment by first endowing buyers with the product. If buyers can be persuaded to take the product home, they will adjust their reference point to include the newly acquired asset. They will then be reluctant to return the product when payment is due, since this will require that they incur a loss.

Framing the consequence of the purchase decision

A frequent advertising strategy used to market high-quality brands is framing the purchase, not in terms of the advantage of buying the high-quality brand (a gain), but in terms of the potential loss associated with not buying it. For example, American Express, for a long time a leader in the sales of travellers cheques, used to frame the risk involved in travelling in a distant location as being unable to get a refund from a less well-known competitor. Not only were the travellers cheques lost, so also was the holiday. Other product categories, however, preserve one's utility and usually cause consumers to think in terms of negative thoughts and potential outcomes. Such categories might include home security systems, insurance, and health products. Framing potential losses is more likely to be effective in these environments because buyers are often concerned with negative consequences.

Bundling gains and losses

Gains and losses have a diminishing effect, as they grow larger relative to the reference point. This has important implications for bundling gains or losses which usually involve bundling or unbundling separate products, prices, or payment in ways that enhance buyers' perceived change in utility. Consequently it is normally helpful to unbundle gains, bundle losses, bundle small losses with larger gains, and unbundle smaller gains from larger losses. Buyers generally perceived their utility to be more positively affected by multiple gains offered separately, because several smaller gains are perceived as having more value than one larger bundled gain. Because several separate losses are perceived as more painful than one larger bundled loss, it is normally better to bundle losses together. By bundling the smaller losses with larger gains, buyers who perceive the price as simply reducing a large gain that has already been subject to diminishing returns, find it less painful than if they see the price as a loss that stands alone. Buyers perceive their utility being less negatively affected if the smaller gain is unbundled from a larger loss, rather than merely reducing the amount of the loss.

Issues in pricing

Establishing a reference price is a key element in understanding pricing. Sellers frequently attempt to influence the buyers' decision by suggesting a reference price. Many companies may establish a high initial list price of an innovation early in the product life cycle in order to establish a higher reference price in buyers' minds; this may also enhance buyers' perceptions of the new product's value. Adding a highly priced version to a product line can raise the reference price by which other products in the line are judged. However, the overuse of price dealing can depreciate buyers' perceptions of the reference price for some branded products. Buyers' perceptions of prices are influenced in three ways; the current prices to which they are exposed, recalled prices which they remember from past exposure, and the context within which the prices are offered.

The influence of current prices

One way to influence the reference price is to control the order in which prices are presented to buyers. Consumers appear to use exposure to earlier prices to develop an initial frame of reference to help to make judgements about later observed prices. In a recent study it was found that subjects who saw prices in descending order (from highest to lowest) were willing to pay more for an item than subjects who saw prices in ascending order (from lowest to highest). The study also found that subjects exposed to descending prices were more likely to purchase more items than the subjects exposed to ascending prices, and were more likely to consider their final purchase price good value (Simonson and Tversky, 1992). The same study found that by adding a higher priced product to the top of a product line made the remaining products appear less expensive because the buyers' reference price increases. Adding a premium product to a product line may not necessarily result in increasing sales of the premium product itself, but it did appear to enhance buyers' perceptions of lower priced products in the product line, as well as influencing low-end buyers to trade up to higher price models. Suppliers suggesting specific reference prices can also influence the reference price. They can be raised, for example, by stating a manufacturer's suggested price, a higher price charged previously, or a higher price charged by a competitor. Although buyers may discount or question the credibility of the suggested prices, their perceptions and behaviours may be favourably influenced.

The influence of past prices

The consumers' reference price is also influenced by recalled prices seen in the past. Past prices have important implications for pricing new products. The price last paid has a particularly strong influence on the reference price because it is more likely to be recalled as a frame of reference than past prices that were observed but not paid. One implication of this is that numerous small price increases for frequently purchased items are more likely to be accepted than infrequent large increases. In a similar way, resistance to price increases for infrequently purchased durable goods is likely to be especially great.

The purchase context

The purchase context is important as a frame of reference that makes the price appear fair or reasonable. One way consumers judge price fairness is to assess the purchase context of the seller as a means of estimating approximately what it cost the seller to deliver the product.

Framing price differences

Prices are frequently expressed with odd endings – 1.99, 19.95, 79.95, rather than round numbers. This suggests that buyers use left-most digits in a price and round up to form a quick reference point to evaluate the actual price. People tend to process price digit information from left to right. In the research referred to earlier, the authors noted that the evidence on odd pricing was mixed. They did find, however, that data collected on the pricing of grocery items indicated that cutting prices to an odd number just below a round one produces a substantially greater effect. They also prepared a simple example that is set out below. Consider the two pairs of prices and quickly answer the question – for which pair of prices is the lower price more of a bargain?

	Higher Price	Lower Price
First Pair	0.89	0.75
Second Pair	0.93	0.79

Figure 2.1 *Framing odd price endings*

The authors argue that most people see the lower price as more of a bargain in the second pair of prices. They do so even though the difference is the same in both pairs and the difference is a greater percentage of the price in the first.

The reason advanced is that most people, attempting to avoid the efforts to calculate the difference, simply compare the columns of prices from left to right. They notice that in the first pair, 7 is just one less than 8 and in the second pair, 7 is two less than 9. Consequently the price difference is greater in the second pair than in the first. Only if the first digits in the first column were the same would they have looked closely at the next column in making a price comparison (Smith and Nagle, 1995). This then explains why retailers often price goods as (for example) 19.99.

If consumers were perfectly rational in their responses to price differences, the same absolute price difference would generate the same response. But consumers appear to frame differences in price in relative terms rather than absolute terms. So, buyers perceive price differences in proportional terms, which means that the perception of a price change depends on the percentage, not the absolute difference, and that there are thresholds above and below a product price at which price changes are noticed or ignored. A series of smaller price increases below the threshold is likely to be more successful than one large increase. Conversely, consumers are likely to respond more to one large price cut below the lower threshold than to a series of smaller successive discounts.

2.3 Consumers' Perceptions of Quality

There are two factors which are contributing to the growing importance of product quality. First is the growth in national incomes. As nations become more prosperous, consumers increasingly wish to consume not just a greater quantity of goods and services but also goods of higher quality. The second factor is the liberalization of world trade and capital regimes. The concomitant globalization of the world economy implies that suppliers located in the developed countries increasingly face competition from suppliers located in low-wage countries. Consequently many firms in the developed world are engaged in a 'flight to quality' – they are repositioning themselves to produce relatively sophisticated products that embody highly skilled labour or cutting-edge technologies – factors of production in which developed countries still enjoy some comparative advantage over the developing world. The newly industrializing countries are giving chase, and attempting to climb the value-added ladder by enhancing the quality of their products, that would permit a transition of these economies from low-wage to high-wage ones. Product quality, consequently, is becoming increasingly important to firms located in developed and newly industrializing countries alike.

We examined consumers' views of the role of quality in the market for domestic appliances (Asch *et al.*, 1998). We found that the top five elements in determining quality were: the brand's reputation for high quality in the product area, good experience with the brand's product, looks, the brand's reputation for high quality for all domestic appliances, and good experience *vis à vis* other products by the brand.

The reputation of the brand for high quality in the product area was the most important element in perceptions of quality. Reputation of the brand in domestic appliances as a whole was also seen to be important in shaping views of perceived quality. Both experience with the brand's product, and experience with other appliances produced by the brand were important determinants of perceived quality. Product-specific experience was found to be more important than experience in the general appliance category as one would expect, but economies of scope in consumer perceptions of quality formed as a result of past experience of a brand's products are evidently quite important.

Physical appearance was very highly correlated with perceived quality. This is somewhat surprising given that the products under study are all experience products, and one would expect that only a limited amount of quality-related information could be gleaned by merely inspecting the product. Consumers, obviously, think otherwise. Recommendations by magazines and by friends/relatives seem more important than recommendations by retail staff. This may be so because magazines and friends are perceived to be disinterested, neutral parties while advice from retail salespeople may be biased. Consumers may also rely on magazines because they provide expert opinion. Reviews in the TV or press did not rank very highly.

The two after-sales elements, namely guarantee and after-sale service, both turn out to be equally important determinants of perceived quality. Clearly, consumers don't just worry about their product going wrong – they are also very concerned about the kind of guarantee and the quality of the after-sales service that the supplier provides if the item is faulty. Consumer perceptions of the quality of guarantee and after-sales service supplied by the brand are highly correlated with consumer perceptions of perceived product quality.

If the brand is advertised as a high quality product, this has a very important influence on perceived quality. The perception of how much the brand advertises in the product area or in domestic appliances also has a significant effect. If the brand is well known in the product area, or in domestic appliances – that also contributes to perceived quality. Advertising of course may contribute to people getting to know the brand.

The innovation record of the supplier as reflected in the continuous upgrading of products enhances consumers' perceptions of quality product. Perceptions concerning the supplier being an experienced player in the product area or in domestic appliances also contribute to perceived quality.

Economies of scope in perception (the perceptual scope factor) are thus again important in the process of perception formation. The manufacturer producing a wide range of products in the product area is also significantly correlated with perceived quality. If the manufacturer is seen to specialize in the product area, this enhances the supplier's quality image. A manufacturer's image of a broader specialization in the supply of domestic appliances also contributes to perceived quality, but less so than the perception of the supplier specializing in the product area. Being perceived as pricing at the higher end of the market is also seen to influence quality perceptions.

In considering factors related to retailer reputation we found that wide availability is correlated with perceived quality. Thus, the fact of the brand being widely acceptable by retailers, may give confidence to consumers in the quality of its products. It is also likely to contribute to greater brand visibility and familiarity, which may also help in this regard. It also helps if the major retailers stock the brand.

It is evident from the research that consumer perceptions of the quality of a brand's product are influenced by a variety of variables, and the effect is stronger of some than of others. The results have important strategic implications for decision-makers in the white goods industry. It suggests how managers can devise strategies for influencing consumer perceptions of product quality. For example, our data suggests that by paying special attention to the issues of looks, recommendations of magazines, after-sales service, guarantee and the nature of advertising, firms can positively influence perceived quality. Good experience with the brand's product and the recommendation of friends are highly important factors, which implies that suppliers must deliver products that meet the quality expectations of their consumers. Economies of scope are again very important: hence a firm that has established a reputation for quality in one product area in domestic appliances gains consumer goodwill in other product areas in the domestic appliance industry. It may thus be a good strategy to actively exploit reputational economies of scope to diversify into other product categories within the white goods industry. Similarly, we point to the importance of continual innovation, and to the involvement of retailers, as devices to influence perceived quality. Some brands have acquired global reputations for excellence and others are geographically limited. Examples of globally recognized names would be Miele, Electrolux, AEG, Whirlpool, GE, Siemens, Bosch. Whereas Hotpoint, Creda, Arthur Martin, Bauknecht would only be instantly recalled in the UK, France and Germany respectively.

The lessons are by no means restricted to the white goods industry. The approach that we have employed here is applicable to any industry that supplies experience products, anywhere in the world. What we are essentially saying is that the strategies that a firm uses for influencing consumer perceptions of product quality should be made in the light of knowledge of how its target consumers come to form perceptions of product quality. Since different products and different markets may significantly differ with respect to the determinants of quality perceptions, we suggest that suppliers should carry out surveys of their target consumers to discover the variables that act as determinants of quality perceptions. Such surveys will then yield information on the basis of which appropriate perception-influencing strategies can be based. If, for example, a survey tells us that the most important determinant of quality perceptions is the degree of advertising, then the supplier should stress the use of an advertising campaign to influence perceived quality. If on the other hand, the role of retailer advice turns out to be extremely important, then it is important to involve retailers in this process. Given that there may be significant complementarities in the use of the various perception-influencing factors, it is important to select and deploy the right mix of perception-influencing instruments, and to do so in a coherent, coordinated fashion. In other words, it is important to take a strategic perspective with respect to the influencing of consumer perceptions regarding product quality.

2.4 Understanding the Properties of Goods and Services

A useful framework for understanding differences between goods and services is a classification of properties developed by economists (Nelson, 1970, 1974, and Darby and Karni, 1973). We can distinguish between three categories of properties in goods and services: *search* qualities, that is those attributes that can be determined before purchase; *experience* qualities which are attributes that can only be discerned after purchase or during consumption; and *credence* qualities which are characteristics that the consumer may find impossible to evaluate even after purchase and consumption. Search qualities might include style, price, fit, feel, hardness, smell, and colour. Experience qualities would include taste and wearability. Products such as cars, clothing, furniture and jewellery are high in search qualities because the attributes can be almost completely determined and evaluated before purchase. Goods and services such as holidays and restaurant meals are high in experience qualities because their attributes cannot be known or assessed until they have been purchased and are being consumed. Examples of offerings high in credence qualities are medical procedures and professional services. Few consumers possess sufficient medical or professional skills to evaluate whether the services were necessary or were performed properly even after they have been prescribed and produced by the seller.

Figure 2.2 looks at goods and services high in search, experience, or credence qualities along a continuum of evaluation ranging from easy to evaluate to difficult to evaluate. Goods high in search qualities are the easiest to evaluate. Goods and services high in experience qualities are more difficult to evaluate, since they must be purchased and consumed before assessment is possible (centre of the continuum). Goods and services high in credence qualities are most difficult to evaluate, because the consumer may be unaware of or may lack sufficient knowledge to appraise whether the offerings satisfy given wants or needs even after consumption. It is notable that the intangibility, heterogeneity, and inseparability of services lead them to possess few search qualities and many experience qualities. Intangibility means services cannot be displayed, physically demonstrated, or illustrated; heterogeneity means that consumers cannot be certain about performance on any given day, even if they use the same service provider on a regular basis. Inseparability of production and consumption means the buyer usually participates in producing the service, thereby affecting the performance and quality of the service. Credence qualities dominate many services, especially those provided by professionals and specialists (for example, lawyers, accountants, medical practitioners).

Because experience and credence qualities dominate in services, consumers employ different evaluation processes than those they use with goods when search qualities dominate. They are also likely to experience the steps in the decision-making process in different orders and at different times from the steps outlined in the buying process discussed later in this chapter. In our view, the key distinction lies between search, experience, and credence goods and services rather than between goods and services as such. In the rest of this chapter we will treat goods and services interchangeably.

2.5 The Buying Decision Process

Consumer decision-making varies with the type of buying decision. There are great differences between acquiring an item high in search qualities (for example, clothing), an experience good or service (for example, a holiday), or a service high in credence qualities (for example, a pension). The more complex and expensive decisions are likely to involve more buyer deliberation and more buying participants. Where consumers are highly involved in a purchase and aware of significant differences between brands they are likely to go through complex buying behaviour. Consumers are highly involved in a purchase when it is expensive, bought infrequently, risky, and highly expressive. Typically they do not know much about the product category and have much to learn. Complex buying behaviour is likely to be

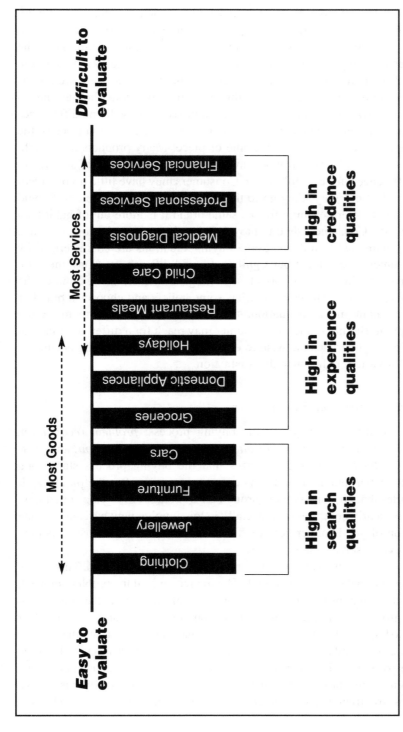

Figure 2.2 *Continuum of evaluation for different types of product (adapted from Zeithaml and Bitner [1996] 'Services Marketing', p.58)*

characterized by a cognitive learning process which involves developing beliefs about the product, then moving towards attitudes, then toward the product, and finally making a deliberate purchase choice. Sometimes the consumer is highly involved in a purchase but sees little differences in the brands. The high involvement is based on the fact that the purchase is expensive, infrequent, and risky. In this case the buyer will shop around to learn what is available, then will buy fairly quickly, because brand differences are not pronounced. The buyer may respond primarily to a good price or the convenience of purchasing at that time or place. Many products are bought under conditions of low consumer involvement in the absence of significant brand differences, for example sugar. Consumers may have little involvement in this product category; they go to the store and reach for the item. Should they happen to keep reaching for the same brand it is more out of habit than brand loyalty. Consumers tend to have low involvement with most low-cost, frequently purchased products. Some buying situations are characterized by low consumer involvement but significant brand differences. Consumers are often involved in a lot of brand switching. Consider, for example, the purchase of biscuits. The consumer has some beliefs and chooses a brand of biscuits without much evaluation, they choose to evaluate them during consumption. But next time the consumer may reach for a different brand out of boredom and perhaps the wish to experiment. Brand switching occurs for the sake of variety rather than dissatisfaction.

Stages in the buying decision process

We can identify five stages in the buying process: *problem recognition, information search, evaluation of alternatives, purchase decision,* and *post-purchase behaviour*. This emphasizes that the buying process starts long before the actual purchase and has consequences long after the purchase. It also implies that consumers pass through all five stages in buying something. But this is clearly not the case, especially in low involvement purchases or the acquisition of goods or services high in credence qualities. Consumers may skip or reverse some of these stages.

The buying process starts with recognition of a problem or need. This can be created by internal or external stimuli. Having recognized the problem or need, the consumer may or may not search for more information. If the consumer's drive is strong, and an affordable gratification object is at hand, the consumer is likely to buy the object then. If not the need may simply be stored in memory. If the consumer undertakes some search activity we can distinguish between two types of search. Firstly, heightened attention, where the consumer simply becomes more receptive to information, by paying attention to advertisements, purchases by friends and conversations about the subject. Secondly the

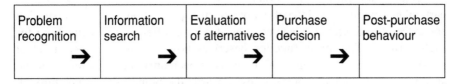

Problem recognition	Information search	Evaluation of alternatives	Purchase decision	Post-purchase behaviour
→	→	→	→	

Figure 2.3 *The five-stage buying process*

consumer may actively search out information, where they look for reading material, engage in other search activities to obtain product information, or contact friends. The amount of search undertaken depends on the strength of the drive and the information initially held, plus of course the ease of obtaining additional information and the value placed upon it. Normally the amount of search activity increases as the consumer moves from decision situations of limited problem solving to extensive problem solving.

There are four groups of consumer information sources:

- Personal sources (family, friends, acquaintances)
- Commercial sources (advertising, sales personnel, dealers, displays)
- Public sources (mass media, consumer organizations)
- Experiential sources (handling, examining, using the product).

The relative influence of the sources varies with the product category and the buyer's characteristics. In general, buyers receive the most information about a product from commercial sources; that is, firm or producer dominated sources. On the other hand, the most effective exposures tend to come from personal sources. Each type of source may perform a somewhat different function in influencing the buying decision. Commercial information normally performs an informing function, and personal sources perform a legitimizing and/or evaluation function.

There are several decision evaluation processes. Most consumer evaluation processes are cognitively oriented – that is, they see the consumer as forming product judgements largely on a conscious and rational basis. Each consumer sees a given product as a bundle of attributes. Consumers vary as to which attributes they consider relevant. They will pay the most attention to those attributes that are connected with their needs. Consumers are also likely to attach different weights to the relevant attributes. So, a distinction can be drawn between the importance of attributes and their salience. Salient attributes are those that come to the consumers' mind when they are asked to think of the product's attributes. Consumers are also likely to develop a set of brand beliefs about where each brand sits on each attribute. The set of beliefs held about a particular brand is known as the brand image. Consumers' beliefs about a particular brand may be at variance with the real attributes owing to their particular experience and the effect of selective perception, selective distortion and selective attention. Consumers may also have different utility functions for each attribute. The utility function describes how consumers expect product satisfaction to vary with alternative levels of each attribute. Consumers arrive at attitudes (judgements, preferences) towards the brand alternatives through some evaluation procedure. They will tend to apply different evaluation procedures to make a choice amongst multi-attribute objects.

Having evaluated the decision the consumer can then form a purchase intention and lead towards buying the preferred item. However, the attitude of others may have influence on the outcome, particularly if the other person's negative attitude towards the preferred alternative is intense, and the consumer is motivated to comply with the other individual's wishes. The purchase intention may also be influenced by unanticipated situational factors, such as that some other purchase may become more urgent, or a friend might report that a similar item or brand was disappointing, or the individual may lose their job. A decision to modify, postpone, or avoid a purchase decision is heavily influenced by perceived risk. Having decided to execute a purchase intention there could then be a number of purchase subdecisions. For example, a choice of brand, then vendor, quantity, timing, and payment method. The decision is not necessarily made in this order. Purchases of everyday products, in contrast, involve fewer of these decisions and much less buyer deliberation.

After purchasing the good or service the consumer will experience some level of satisfaction or dissatisfaction. The buyer's satisfaction is a function of the closeness between their expectations of the product/service and its perceived performance. If it matches expectations the consumer is likely to be satisfied. If the product exceeds them then the buyer is likely to be highly satisfied. If the product falls short of expectations the consumer will be dissatisfied. The consumer's satisfaction or dissatisfaction with the product will influence subsequent behaviour. If the consumer is satisfied then they may purchase the same good or service on the next occasion. The satisfied consumer will also tend to say good things about the item to others.

2.6 A Developing Framework for Understanding Consumers

We have covered a great deal of ground on very complex subject matter so far in this chapter. We will now try to draw the various strands together by developing a comprehensive model that provides insights into how consumers may behave. We will do this in two ways. First, we will revisit

Figure 2.2. This you may recall set out a range of goods and services on a continuum from easy to evaluate to difficult to evaluate. This continuum was established by identifying the categories of properties (search, experience and credence) in a variety of goods and services. We will now add to this our understanding of how consumers make buying decisions. The question here is whether or not the buying decision is complex, and hence has a high degree of involvement on the part of the consumer. That is, the purchase is likely to be expensive, bought infrequently, risky, and highly expressive. Purchases that are made frequently and are of low cost tend to have low involvement by the consumer. Figure 2.4 brings together these two dimensions and uses the goods and services initially identified merely as high in search, experience and credence qualities to illustrate the point.

Customer Involvement

	High in Search Qualities	High in Experience Qualities	High in Credence Qualities
HIGH	Jewellery Furniture	Child Care Holidays Restaurant Meals Domestic Appliances	Medical Diagnosis Professional Services Financial Services (e.g. a mortgage)
LOW	Clothing	Groceries	Financial Services (e.g. credit cards)

Easy to Evaluate ⟵——————————⟶ *Difficult to Evaluate*

Figure 2.4 *Understanding customer choice*

From this we can see that jewellery, furniture and clothing are high in search qualities, that is those attributes which can be determined and evaluated before purchase such as style, price, colour, and so on. Because the purchase of jewellery or furniture is likely to be infrequent and highly expressive, as well as expensive, these two items have high customer involvement. Clothing on the other hand, particularly basic items such as undergarments, socks, or shirts, which are often sold in boxes or pre-wrapped ready for purchase, are likely to be purchased frequently, are probably of comparatively low cost, and so have low customer involvement. We noted earlier in this chapter that goods and services such as holidays and restaurant meals are high in experience qualities because their attributes cannot be known or assessed until they have been purchased and are being consumed. Similar considerations apply to domestic appliances such as refrigerators and washing machines. In a case of a service such as childcare we will be unable to ascertain how good the service is until our child or children return home happy. Once more, because of the nature of these particular goods and services, customer involvement is likely to be high. Clearly groceries are goods which are high in experience qualities. Because they are bought frequently and because each individual item is of low value they have little customer involvement. Indeed, should we purchase a basic grocery item, such as a breakfast cereal or biscuits, which we do not like, it is not a major concern for us to replace it with another product the following week.

Services high in credence qualities have characteristics which we may find impossible to evaluate after purchase and use, or divide between those with low involvement and those with high involvement. Because they are frequent transactions, some financial services like retail banking and car insurance have low consumer involvement. Those services with high consumer involvement are likely to be expensive, infrequent and perhaps involve more risk (just how good is that surgeon, consultant?). So, such services would include the examples above of the use of consultancy firms, medical procedures, and some financial services such as acquiring a mortgage.

We return to this model or framework in Chapter 7 when we consider which goods and services appear to be suitable for sale and possibly delivery using the Internet.

In conclusion we return to our opening statement. Consumer behaviour is a very complex subject which is influenced by a wide variety of factors. Retailers can and do influence consumers, but the effect on consumers is very dependent on their backgrounds – family, social and educational. So it is a complicated picture that we need to understand before we go on to look at markets, government and other influences.

3

The Nature of Markets

In this chapter we will address the central issue of how markets work and what influences the nature of competition across the whole value chain of a product or service. The chapter starts by introducing a framework which helps us to understand the nature of competition, and to identify the key determinants of the nature of competition in a market or industry. Following this we identify factors or influences which shape the way in which a market develops. We also consider the different stages of development of the industry. We conclude the chapter by looking at an example and flagging some key issues for consideration in subsequent chapters.

3.1 Analysing Industries and Markets

In order to understand the industry or a market we first need to identify what market or markets we are interested in. As we saw in the previous chapter we should therefore be clear about the needs of the customers and who it is that customers see as the competition. The key point here is that it is the buyer of the product or service that determines and defines the market. Consider the case of a business selling used cars. The firm has a certain amount to spend on advertising and promotion. There are a number of alternatives available. For example, they could advertise in a local newspaper, they could buy advertising space on local radio, rent some hoardings, or purchase off-peak time on regional TV. For this particular business these are just some of the alternatives, having due regard to costs and effectiveness, that could be used to meet promotional and advertising needs. So, if we were responsible for managing the local radio station we would need to consider that the competitors for advertising revenues were not just other local radio stations but all other forms of media in that town or region. In order to identify in more detail the markets that we are considering we must first identify the needs of the buyers and then identify competition from their perspective.

Having established an acceptable definition of the market we are interested in, we can analyse systematically the competitive forces that are influencing this market. Firms rarely operate in just one, clearly defined, homogeneous market. Usually a firm operates in several markets, and within each market there are likely to be distinct segments of demand – segments being groups of buyers with similar needs. For example, a French cycle manufacturer may be competing in the home market as well as exporting to a number of countries in Europe. Within the French market there may be a number of segments of demand, for example adult racing bikes, bikes for girls aged three to six and so on. It can be useful to try to assess the European cycle market as a whole (using the techniques explained below) but it is usually necessary to follow up this broad assessment with analyses of specific markets and segments within markets.

Porter (1980) has constructed a useful framework for analysing the structure of an industry (Figure 3.1). For our purposes an industry is defined as a group of firms producing similar products or services for the same market, for example bicycle manufacturers serving the European market. Porter's approach concentrates on the competitive forces operating in the industry, the outcome of the analysis being an assessment of the nature of competition in the industry. The real benefit of this approach is that it forces us to take a broader perspective of competition than would typically be the case.

Porter argues that five competitive forces operate in an industry, which together determine the nature of competition. The five forces are:

- Rivalry among existing firms
- The threat of new entrants
- The bargaining power of buyers
- The bargaining power of suppliers
- The threat from substitute products or services.

We will briefly consider each of these elements in turn.

Rivalry among existing firms

This refers to the intensity of competitive behaviour in the industry. Are firms continually seeking to outmanoeuvre their rivals through price cuts, new product innovations, advertising, credit deals, promotional campaigns and so on? Or is there little competitive activity, the incumbent firms being content to stick with their share of the market, none of them willing to risk upsetting the balance of the industry by, say, instigating a price war? There are a number of factors that together determine the intensity of rivalry in industry.

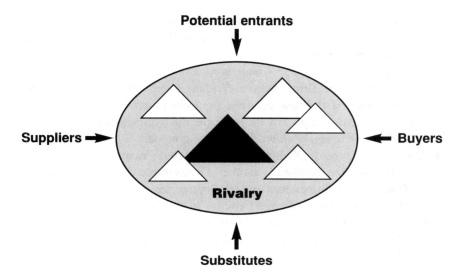

Figure 3.1 *The five competitive forces*

- *Slow growth in demand.* If demand slows, firms can only maintain past growth rates by gaining market share from competitors. This tends to intensify rivalry as firms battle for greater share through price cuts or other attempts to boost sales.
- *Declining demand.* Declining demand will lead to further intensification of competitive activity, particularly if there are exit barriers in the industry. Exit barriers (which makes firms reluctant to leave the industry) can take the form of a large investment in capital equipment that has no other use, the lack of transferable skills (organizational and managerial) and the real cost of plant closure (redundancy, decommissioning and so on).
- *Potential advantages from economies of scale or experience.* If there are substantial advantages to be gained from having a higher relative share of the market (which enables the firm to exploit economies of scale and to benefit from accumulating experience at a faster rate than rivals) then rivalry is likely to be intense. If there are first-mover advantages (for example launching a new technology such as the Sony Walkman) this may also lead to more intense competition.
- *High fixed costs.* If the cost structure of the industry is such that there are high fixed cost components (and low marginal costs) then firms will be under intense pressure to produce at or near full capacity. So if demand

falls off firms will use price cuts and other weapons to maintain sales. Similar behaviour can occur in industries with highly demand-sensitive products, for example airline seats.

- *Unpredictable and diverse competitors*. If the industry is made up of a diverse group of firms then individual behaviour is likely to be unpredictable. If the new entrants are from other countries, or other industries that do not play by the rules, their maverick behaviour is likely to lead to an extremely volatile competitive arena.
- *Low switching costs*. Switching costs are costs incurred by the buyer moving from one supplier to another. For example if an airline with an all-Boeing fleet moves to a mixed Boeing/Airbus fleet it is likely to incur additional costs of crew training, spares inventories and so on. If switching costs are low in an industry, buyers are able to switch between suppliers without incurring a penalty, which will encourage firms to poach buyers from their rivals.

The threat of new entrants

When new firms enter an industry they bring additional capacity. If demand does not increase to absorb this additional capacity, the new entrants would have to compete for share of the existing demand. To gain entry they may either compete with lower prices or with added features or quality (or both). The net effect of these new entries will probably be to lower the overall level of profitability in the industry. Entry is deterred by the presence of barriers to entry, which can stem from several sources:

- *Economies of scale*. If there are major cost advantages to be gained from operating at a large scale then new entrants will either have to match the scale of the incumbents (which might be a risky move) or suffer lower margins. Scale economies can exist in production, advertising, purchasing, research and development, and after-sales service.
- *Experience benefits*. Low unit costs can be achieved by accumulated learning (for example finding more efficient ways of making the product), which, if significant, will place new entrants at a cost disadvantage.
- *Access to know-how*. Patents will protect firms from new entrants, and access to process knowledge and particular skills can make entry difficult.
- *Customer loyalty*. Customers may have preferred brands (supported by heavy advertising) or they may have strong relationships with their existing suppliers that they are reluctant to break. New entrants would have to persuade customers that it is worth incurring these disadvantages when switching to their products. So switching costs act as a barrier to entry.

- *Capital costs of entry.* If these are large they will limit the number of potential entrants. Capital costs of entry include setting up the production facilities, research and development costs, establishing dealers/servicing networks, and advertising and promotion expenses.
- *Access to distribution channels.* For example it would be difficult for an unknown firm to persuade the major grocery retailers to take their products. In order to do this the new entrant may have to offer large discounts to the wholesaler or retailer.

The bargaining power of buyers

Buyers may have considerable bargaining power for a variety of reasons, particularly when:

- There are few buyers and they purchase in large quantities
- The buyers have low switching costs
- Buyers face many sellers who are relatively small
- The item being purchased is not an important input for the buyer.

Examples of powerful buyer relationships include Marks & Spencer and the UK clothing industry. Most government departments of defence are also powerful buyers in relation to suppliers of military equipment. Here buying power is highly concentrated, and if the seller fails to gain an order it can have severe implications for a firm's survival.

More generally, when buyers are faced with many alternatives and few costs are involved in switching from one supplier to another, even though an individual buyer has no power (for example the purchase of a chocolate bar), buyers collectively do have power. If prices rise or product quality declines consumers will readily shift their custom elsewhere.

The bargaining power of suppliers

Suppliers can exert economic power over the firms in industry when:

- The input is important to the buyers
- Buyers have high switching costs
- There are few feasible alternative sources of supply (and making the component inhouse would be uneconomic)
- Buying firms are not important customers of the suppliers.

Examples of powerful supplier–buyer relationships are gas suppliers into the glass container industry and microchip suppliers to the computer industry. A broad definition of suppliers would take in suppliers of capital and skills. If an industry is dependent on particular skilled people these individuals can bargain up their pay levels. If suppliers are powerful they can increase the price of inputs, thus extracting potential profits from the industry. If firms in an industry face powerful suppliers and powerful buyers, profits will be severely squeezed as input cost increases cannot be passed on in higher prices to buyers.

The threat from substitute products or services

Industries are usually defined in terms of the product or services they provide. Thus we have the aluminium can industry, the sugar industry, the pizza restaurant industry. Using these product or service based definitions enables us to identify groups of firms doing similar things who we could assume are in competition with each other. However if we define industries from the buyers perspective we might come up with different sets of firms who do not provide the same type of product or service but who nevertheless meet the same type of buyer needs.

The buyer who likes sweet coffee might consider that manufacturers of sugar and those of artificial sweeteners are in direct competition. A father shopping at around lunchtime might see his need to feed his three children being met by a pizza restaurant, a takeaway hamburger or sandwiches from the delicatessen. Manufacturers of diet drinks might consider aluminium cans, plastic bottles and cardboard containers as alternative ways of packaging their products.

Substitute products or services are alternative ways of meeting buyers needs. So if we use the product-based definition of the industry, the pizza restaurant industry is facing threats from substitutes such as hamburger restaurants and takeaways. If such substitutes are perceived to be viable and acceptable ways of meeting buyers, needs then the threat from substitutes is high. The effect on the pizza restaurant industry of those close and acceptably priced alternatives is a limit being placed on price increases and hence profitability.

As we have already argued, defining the boundaries of an industry is more an art than a science. If an overly narrow product-based definition is used there is a risk that our analysis will miss critical aspects of the competitive environment. Some industries are geographically fragmented, with each locality having just one or two producers, for example Quarry stone, cinemas, regional newspapers. In most respects these fragmented firms have little to do with each other; they tend not to compete for the same customers and they face different local conditions. To consider them as rivals would probably be a mistake. To return to our pizza restaurant, a more appropriate industry definition would probably include at least the hamburger restaurants as rivals rather than substitutes.

Advantages of the five forces framework

The main benefit of using this technique is that it provides a structure to think about the competitive arena. Each force can be examined using the checklist set out above; some aspects will be highly relevant to the industry, some irrelevant. There is evidence that by working through this analysis in a systematic way useful insights can be gained into the nature of the industry (Wolfe and Asch 1992). Usually it is appropriate to do several industry analyses. The first will be for the industry as a whole (for example the European packaging machinery industry); subsequent analyses would focus on segments of the industry (high-speed packaging systems, cartons). Analysing the industry as a whole provides a broad understanding of the key forces operating in the industry. More focused segment analyses help us understand better the determinants of competitive behaviour in particular parts of the market. As such, the five forces analysis helps us to make a broader and more comprehensive appraisal of the competitive forces in our industry (or industries). It is typically carried out on the current situation in the industry. Although this is useful we really need to project our thinking forward to try and establish how the market may evolve in the future. If we can identify these dynamic forces and if they can be extrapolated into the future, we may be able to shed some light on to how competition may develop.

3.2 Industry Development

It should be clear from our understanding of the five forces that the most important determinant of competitiveness is the state of demand; is it growing or declining? The concept of the industry lifecycle has been developed to analyse key trends in an industry. Different competitive circumstances can be identified at particular stages of the lifecycle. We shall consider briefly three broad phases of the industry life cycle: the emerging industry, the maturing industry and the declining industry (Porter 1980).

The emerging industry

The early stages in industry evolution are characterized by the absence of any rules of the game. This refers to the accepted ways of competing in industry. For example, the accepted rules in an established industry might be that firms compete through superior packaging and heavy TV advertising; that all competitors offer a full line of products; and heavy discounts are given to major retailers; that after-sales service is subcontracted. In the emerging stages of an industry, rules such as these have yet to be established.

Consequently the early stages of the industry life cycle tend to have the following features:

- Many different ways of competing.
- Poor information on customers and their needs, and on competitors.
- Uncertainty about technologies (no stages have been set for product design; different production technologies are explored).
- High initial unit costs, but a potential for massive reductions in production costs through experience and scale.
- Many new entrants, leading to a large number of small firms.
- Shortages of key supplies (skilled staff, components).

The e-commerce industry developing on the Internet has most of the above characteristics.

The maturing industry

If demand continues to grow the industry will progress from the emerging phrase towards maturity. The most obvious change in the industry is that competitive behaviour is now informed by the rules of the game. In some industries it is clear how these rules have come about. For example the entry of IBM into the personal computer industry was the point at which the rules for competing were set. Because of IBM's dominance in other sectors of the industry, its entry into personal computers had the effect of setting the industry standard. Prior to IBM's entry there were many ways of competing (different hardware, operating systems, software packages); after its entry the rules of the game were essentially to clone the IBM personal computer and compete on price.

In most industries, however, these rules are not established in so obvious a fashion. Accepted ways of competing emerge almost unnoticed over a period of many years. But these rules of the game become so established that they are unchallenged; they become the norm in the industry. It is during the transition from emergence to maturity that the evolution of the rules takes place.

The transition to maturity is also characterized by the slowdown in the rate of growth of demand. This leads to increasingly intense competitive behaviour as firms try to maintain historic growth rates. In the period of slowing growth incumbent firms can only sustain growth rates above the industry rate by taking share from competitors. The combination of the establishment of the rules of the game and slowing industry growth results in an intensification of rivalry within an understood competitive formula.

Firms often sell to more experienced buyers who demand higher service levels and lower prices. Hence attention may shift from product development and the establishment of volume production facilities towards service based sources of differentiation and an internal emphasis on cost control. Firms may struggle to cope with the demands of higher quality levels and low costs, leading to some leaving the industry or being taken over by more efficient rivals.

The global domestic appliance and the motor car industries are but two examples of industries which are mature and demonstrate most of the features identified above.

The declining industry

It may be difficult to detect whether a downturn in demand is the beginning of the end of an industry or a temporary problem caused by the business cycle. A true decline could be brought about by, for example, a change in technology (electronic replacing mechanical calculators; compact discs replacing tapes and vinyl records), changes in needs and tastes (away from eating meats and high fat foods) or demographic shifts (declining birth rates). If incumbent firms believe the downturn to be temporary they are likely to try to weather the storm, and to make sure they are in good shape to benefit from the anticipated upturn.

The ease with which costs can be managed downwards to reflect lower levels of activity will determine the intensity of rivalry in this phase. If firms cannot adjust their costs due to a high fixed cost element then price competition will be intense as firms fight to maintain sales levels and hence capacity utilization.

If the decline is gradual this may permit firms to withdraw from the industry in a more orderly fashion; but it may also send confusing signals to some firms that the decline is only a temporary problem. Rapid decline is unambiguous and management cannot argue about the future prognosis for the industry. This should lead to a dramatic loss of capacity with the industry. As discussed above, a key determinant to the intensity of rivalry in this phase is the existence of exit barriers. In addition to the barriers established through the firm having specialized assets, and the out-of-pocket costs of closure, there are other, psychological, barriers to exit. These include reluctance to relinquish a belief that things will improve, and a belief that there is nowhere else for the firm to go so it may as well stay and fight it out.

Other driving forces in the industry

Although the major growth phases in industry exert a very strong influence over the nature of competition, there are other forces, not necessarily associated with life cycle phases, that must be considered.

- *Changing needs*. New segments of demand with particular requirements can emerge in an industry. Firms that fail to identify these segments may be outmanouvred by others who tailor their products and services to meet these needs. Buyer preferences may shift from expensive, highly tailored products to standardized cheaper versions. Consumers may undergo attitude shifts that force firms to change their products or services, for example concerns for the environment, animal testing.
- *Product innovation*. At the industry level, product innovation can have the effect of rejuvenating a mature industry. For example the video recorder industry has experienced a slowing of growth as the market reaches saturation. The market may be rejuvenated by technical innovations that encourage existing owners to upgrade their recorders, for example the introduction of stereo or enhanced TV picture quality.
- *Marketing innovation*. Although the core product or services might remain the same, innovations in the way the market is reached can result in major shifts in the structure of the industry. For example, personal computers might be sold from the Internet; law firms could advertise on the TV; there could be vertical integration of manufacturing with retailing, and *vice versa*.
- *New competitors*. New entrants from, for example, other countries can radically change competitive behaviour in an industry. They can bring about a different competitive formula that challenges the established rules of the game.
- *The rate of diffusion of know-how*. The speed at which new technologies, operating systems or product innovations are spread through the industry can determine the pace of innovation. Easily imitable innovations can lead to a continual process of innovation among firms to the gaining of shortlived advantages, but then having to move on again (whilst continually incorporating the improvements made by other firms).
- *Changes in the cost structures of the industry*. Shifts in economies of scale and experience curves can lead to the radical restructuring of an industry. Cost advantages built up over years of accumulated experience may be wiped out by changing production technology – the same levels of quality can be achieved at lower costs by the purchase of a new machine. Similarly a change in economies of scale, whereby huge cost advantages can be gained by using very large scale plants, could lead to dramatic battles for market share and to acquisitions as firms seek to achieve the required volumes.
- *Changes in industry structure*. Earlier we noted the extent to which the structure of an industry is affected by the industry life cycle. Although identifying an industry's position in the life cycle is difficult, it may be worth trying to do this if it helps to predict broad changes in the structure

of the industry. More detailed trends may also be identifiable. Some driving forces in the industry, for example product or process innovations, changes in experience curves, economies of scale, rate of diffusion of know-how, will be strongly affected by technological developments. Anticipating the nature and pace of these developments provides insight into how the structure of the industry and the bases of competition may change in the future. So a comprehensive analysis of the competitive environment should involve approaching the basic questions – what changes in demand, competitive behaviour and industry structure are likely to emerge? – from two directions. Firstly, we need to understand these three aspects of the competitive environment, after which the future evolution of the industry can be mapped. The second stage would be to use the techniques explored above. This more structured approach could then be used to modify and challenge the experience based approach.

3.3 Understanding Competition

Having considered how to analyse an industry we now need to place that into the context of how we can understand the nature of competition in a series of industries. We can view the process of delivering a product or service to an end user market as a sequence of discrete value chains (see Figure 3.2). Each discrete chain has its own value adding activities and its own margin to make on these activities. The sequence can also be thought of as one complete industry or market need value system, where the sum of all discreet value chain margins equals the total system margin. We can use Figure 3.2 to illustrate a number of points using the manufacture and sale of personal computers as an example.

Figure 3.2 is a simplified representation of the manufacture and sale of personal computers (PCs). In Figure 3.2 we have simply categorized the end user market into three distinct segments. We have identified them as professional (which relates to the segments which purchase large numbers of PCs, for example major organizations in the public and private sector), education (for example schools, colleges, universities), and small office and home (individual consumers and very small enterprises). Each of these segments has different needs. For example, the professional segment will tend to buy PCs in large numbers and may have a requirement for very specific configurations and set-up for the equipment that it purchases. It will also, because of the nature and size of its business, use particular distribution networks, for example it may use dealers or value added retailers. Given the size of their purchases and the nature of their organizations there will be a

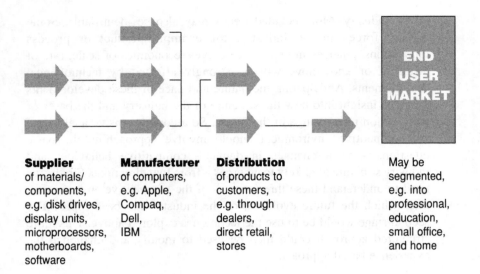

Figure 3.2   *Sequence of value chains: a value system*

professional buying function which will deal with the purchase of PCs. The small office and home customer on the other hand may purchase a single PC from his or her nearest retail outlet. As we saw in the previous chapter, the end users' previous experience will have a major influence on the type of channel used to acquire a PC. For example, if they have previous experience of the product – that is, it is a replacement item – then their relationship with and choice of channel is likely to be quite different from an end user for whom this is a first purchase. This of course then complicates a consideration of competition between those who seek to serve the end user market. For example, if an individual is seeking to purchase a PC she may consider not only well-known retail stores but also some of the smaller dealerships. She may also be tempted to purchase direct from the manufacturer when this is an option.

The comparative size of the channel, in relation to the manufacturer, will determine the comparative buying power that the store or dealer has. As we saw earlier, if the retailer for example takes a comparatively large proportion of output or commands a relatively significant share of the end user segment then they are likely to have considerable influence over the price and possibly specification of the product that they wish to sell. The development of retailer power in Europe over the last 20 years has been one factor which has spurred PC manufacturers into developing a direct channel to end users, so cutting out the retailer and their margin. We will discuss in Chapter 7 the likely influence that the development of sales over the Internet may have, particularly in relation to the balance of power between manufacturers and the distribution channels.

A manufacturer of PCs would need to consider not only the degree of rivalry between manufacturers but also the balance of power between themselves and the distribution channels they use, which we have just discussed. We also need to consider the relative balance of power and hence control between a manufacturer and the suppliers (illustrated in Figure 3.2) from whom they purchase the various elements needed for a PC. In this particular industry some suppliers are very powerful, for example, Intel who supply the microprocessors and Microsoft who supply the operating systems and software. Interestingly, both of these companies also advertise and promote themselves direct to end users (for example, 'Intel inside'), in order to create 'pull-through demand' in the same way that the manufacturers of Lycra and Spandex do in the clothing market. In the PC industry this combination of Intel chips and Microsoft software has become known as the WinTel standard; both of these companies, by virtue of their monopoly position, are able to effectively dictate terms to PC manufacturers. Other suppliers to the PC makers do not have the same degree of influence.

Illustration 3.1

Dixons Accused of PC Profiteering

A spokeswoman for Intel confirmed that its chief executive had said at an industry trade fair that 'Dixons charges ridiculous margins'. He was backed by the Vice-President of the Intel Architecture Business Group, who said: 'Dixons has classic channel presence and can determine what gets sold at what price.'

A spokesman for Dixons, which also owns Currys and PC World, said the group 'couldn't make any sense of the comments ... Intel is interpreting its drop in market share in our stores as a problem with the market'. Intel currently controls about 85–90 per cent of the chip market but is facing strong competition from another manufacturer, AMD, which introduced its K6 chip earlier this year.

But the consumers association said the public should be 'concerned'. 'There appears to be more evidence to support this and we are concerned that UK consumers are getting a rew deal,' said a senior policy researcher at the association. 'Dixons controls over half of the high-street distribution of PCs and they seem to be using its enormous market power to keep prices to consumers high.'

Dixons responded by saying that its share of the domestic market overall is 15 per cent and added that it introduced its PC for under £500 last month. 'The market is extremely competitive and the UK consumer is getting good value for money,' a spokesman said.

An analyst at the Inteco Corporation said that, at present, the UK consumer was paying an average £1230 a computer, the French consumer about the same but Germans £950 on average. 'The major reason is that the UK is still a high income market and can bear higher prices,' he said. 'The UK is also more dominated by known brands whose prices are high. In Germany there are local low-cost assemblers who put out PCs without brands on.'

Source: The Independent, 20 November 1998

The example in Illustration 3.1 indicates that even a dominant supplier to PC manufacturers, such as Intel, may have a problem with an ultimate channel to the end user, in this case the retailer. Intel appears to be concerned that the retailer is charging too high a price for a product which contains its microprocessors. So, although Intel is able to exert considerable influence over PC manufacturers, it may still take issue with a channel to the ultimate customer. Whether or not Dixons charges too high a price for a PC, there is some evidence that consumers in the UK and in Europe tend to pay higher prices for products than US consumers. This example also illustrates that whoever 'owns' the end user is likely to be in a very powerful position. In this particular example the British Office for Fair Trading (OFT) cleared personal computer retailers after a ten month investigation. The apparent differences in price between the UK and other European countries resulted from British consumers' preference for higher specification machines.

So, in reviewing the nature of competition across the supply chain in the PC industry we can see that computer manufacturers face fierce competition from other manufacturers in an industry which is characterized also by concentration on both the supply and demand sides. It is hardly surprising therefore that despite the high historic growth rates in the industry, profits are hard to find. The comparative profitability of retailers for example, or more particularly Intel and Microsoft, is quite marked.

If we consider the overall system that we have just been discussing, we can begin to see the logic for companies at any point in the value chain seeking to integrate either forwards or backwards. So, a PC manufacturer may seek to integrate forward, for example by acquiring part of the distribution channel, such as a retailer or dealer network. Alternatively, or additionally, they may also seek to integrate backwards by acquiring a supplier. This would enable them to gain control over more elements of the system in order to reconfigure value adding activities across the whole value system. This might reduce significantly the cost base, increase the perceived value to end users or downstream processes, so earning a premium. Gaining more direct access to the end user market may alter perceptions such that new or improved uses for the end product may be stimulated, increasing demand and/or consumer prices. Whichever way a firm integrates the balance of power is likely to be altered. In seeking to extend power and influence along the value system it is not necessary to acquire other elements of the chain. The notion of influence is important, as a number of examples suggest that companies are increasingly finding subtle and sophisticated ways of achieving integration along the value system without necessarily acquiring fellow processors.

For example, many major Japanese companies are renowned for the close relationships they have with their suppliers through such mechanisms as 'Just in Time' supply of production contracts, proactive supplier quality practices and specifications and so on. Although often described as 'win-win'relationships, there is little doubt that these mechanisms increase the power of these companies along their value systems. In the UK, food retailers and clothing retailers (for example Tesco and Marks & Spencer) are renowned for the influence they exert over their suppliers. Another example would be the shifting balance of power between travel agents and tour operators. This changed significantly with the introduction of information systems controlled by the tour operator into the offices of travel agents in the early 1980s. This allowed tour operators to influence the booking procedure significantly to their advantage and gain more control over the distribution channels without having to acquire travel agents. For airline operators the advent of Internet technology is again altering the balance of power in their distribution chain as they are able to offer ticketing direct to passengers rather than using alternative distribution channels such as travel agencies.

Electronic point of sale (EPOS) gathered in retail outlets has enabled some suppliers to gain advantage by better establishing consumer demand (Benetton used such information to switch their dyeing processes at short notice from predicted fashion colours to those actually demanded), to keep better track of stocks held, to reduce the need for large buffer stocks. EPOS systems have enabled improved efficiency and shortened cycle times so reducing the need for working capital investment. This sort of information has significantly altered the balance of power in favour of large retailers, and many now insist on their suppliers installing compatible systems, so increasing suppliers' switching costs. As a final example, important trading partners have often made 'trading investments' in each other to secure, for example, a seat on the board, relative security and loyalty of supply, a defensive bulwark should a competitor threaten to acquire their vertical partner.

If we think of value systems and sequences of business value chains we can also see that companies may benefit from horizontal integration. This is most likely to lead more companies to extend lateral linkages between parallel value systems. In this way a firm can seek to increase sales from their existing products by finding ways to supply them in new end user markets (for example selling PCs into the home as not only a computer but also a communications device and a games machine). This is notably the case when companies seek to expand into new geographic markets. A linkage could also be made by introducing products from other markets to the markets that the company currently serves. A recent example of horizontal integration has been the American retailer, Wal-Mart's, acquisitions of other supermarkets in Europe (for example, Asda in the UK in mid 1999).

Consider Illustration 3.2. This brief extract indicates how food retailing has concentrated in Europe during the last decade. Using a 'quick and dirty'

Illustration 3.2

Selling Power

European retailing is now big business. Ranked by turnover, 18 of the top 100 European companies are retailers. Nine of the world's top ten food retailers are European, but America's Wal-Mart is by far the world's biggest. Europe's biggest retailer, Germany's Metro group, had a turnover of US$52.1 bn last year; Britain's biggest, Tesco is the country's fourth largest firm. Retailing is also becoming more concentrated. Europe's top ten grocers had a market share of 36 per cent in 1997 up from 28 per cent in 1992. In Britain the top five grocers had 64 per cent of the market in 1996.

Top five grocers' share of national markets, per cent	1988	1996
Britain	53	64
France	41	52
Germany	27	41
Spain	20	25

Large retail chains can take advantage of economies of scale in storage, logistics and the like. Big retailers can secure better deals from manufacturers. These savings should be passed on to consumers – so long as they risk losing customers to their rivals if they raise prices. Many retailers now dwarf their suppliers. Retailers may thus be able to impose unfavourable terms on the suppliers that restrict competition. Indeed, even the biggest manufacturers now have to pay for space on supermarket shelves.

This often benefits retailers more than it does consumers. Retail margins are rising, particularly in Britain. OECD figures show that European prices remain much higher than America's. True, the Internet may eventually dent retailers' margins. But for now competition is often sorely lacking. Prime locations are scarce, so stores often have a local monopoly. Retail chains with an established distribution network have a big advantage over any potential new competitors. And retailers are no longer just sales outlets. Consumers may sometimes care as much about where they shop as about what they buy. Shops increasingly provide extra services, such as child-care facilities. And retailers' proprietary brands are gaining ground at manufacturers' expense.

Antitrust authorities have plenty of catching up to do. To start with, they could reconsider some of the blanket exemptions from European competition law enjoyed by, for instance, car showrooms. They can also review licensing and planning restrictions that often buttress retailers' local monopolies. Supermarkets have long sold themselves as shoppers' friends. Trustbusters should set little store by such claims.

Source: The Economist, 10 April 1999.

five forces framework we can identify key aspects of competition in food retailing across Europe. The first element in determining the nature of competition in this industry is the small number (relatively speaking) of large retailers. So, one strand of thought might be that competition is intense between these firms. However, as Illustration 3.2 indicates, it appears that food supermarkets may well benefit from local monopolies as competition is effectively local and localized. Competition between firms is perhaps governed by the number and type of retail outlets and associated selling space than directly between retail outlets. In addition, the outlets offer added value by providing additional services (for example childcare facilities). Dobson and Waterson (1999) argue that consumers' reasons for preferring one particular store to another, apart from price, include location, accessibility, layout, ambience, product range, sales personnel and service. They argue that differentiation among retailers dampens competition and that differentiation exists for large and small stores alike. Consequently, retailers put great effort into distinguishing their service from that of competitors. Large multi-product chain stores have developed own brands to attract customers to their stores to buy, and continue to buy, goods from them rather than from rivals. Large retailers have thus been heavy users of advertising to promote their brands.

The ability of potential new entrants to enter the market is also severely limited by the use of planning constraints by the central and local governments. That is, planning approvals for new large stores and shopping complexes in the UK, for example, are very limited. This is one example of how an over-arching regulatory framework can influence competition at a local, regional, or national level (we will consider the influence of regulatory frameworks in more detail in Chapter 4). One important consequence of this is to give incumbent retailers the advantages associated with having the best locations. Incumbency advantages are also reinforced by economies of size and scope, which give large retailers a cost advantage. Increasing returns arise because fixed costs can be spread over high output levels and variable costs also fall with scale, particularly when economies are made from buying in bulk. Economies of scope in retailing can also arise from using common display, storage and sales recording facilities for a variety of products, so allowing fixed cost to be spread across different product lines. Dobson and Waterson (1999) provide compelling evidence for the considerable consolidation that has taken place. They note that in the UK sales of fast moving consumer goods by supermarkets were 20 per cent in 1960 and 85 per cent by 1997, with the top 2 per cent of stores controlling 47 per cent of grocery sales. The number of grocery retail outlets fell from over 140 000 to below 40 000 in the UK during 1960–97, from 152 000 to

41 700 during 1968–94 in France, and from 212 700 to 69 000 in the former West Germany during 1955–89. They note that in southern Europe the trend is similar. They conclude that the decline in the total number of retail grocers and the development of chain store groups, at the expense of independent retailers, caused a sharp rise in national concentration levels.

Probably the most powerful element in determining the nature of competition is the influence that large food retailers have over their suppliers. As manufacturers compete for access to selling space in even more concentrated retail markets, it is retailers who increasingly dictate terms and conditions of trade. Large retailers not only negotiate volume discounts from suppliers, but they obtain other benefits from them: examples include charging suppliers 'slotting allowances' to access prime shelf space, and 'market development funds' to pay for local cooperative advertising and in-store displays.

Competitive pressure on suppliers is further enhanced by retailers own-label brands that are vigorously promoted within the store. Powerful retailers now use closely controlled 'preferred suppliers', who can in turn subcontract production creating a supply hierarchy. For the retailer, risk is shifted to the preferred suppliers who are responsible for delivery and quality while receiving very narrow margins. Consequently these retailer–supply relationships are highly asymmetric. The retailers can exercise control over the production process (usually dictating the technology required and providing exact product specifications) without carrying the burden of ownership (that is, quasi-integration). Retail branding has become particularly important for retailers with similar product ranges to rivals, particularly in grocery and clothes retailing. It has the double benefits of differentiating services on the selling side and providing bargaining power on the buying side to counter the selling power brand of manufacturers. The manufacturers' position is especially weak if retailers develop own-label products, which break the manufacturers' link with consumers that has been built up through direct appeal, typically through advertising. The service reputation of retailers means that their own brands commonly command a significant premium over 'no brands', and own-label product can also undercut leading brands. Selling own-label product is an important form of brand extension for retailers, reinforcing the stores image and building customer loyalty. By using buying power to obtain own-label goods at the lowest possible price, retail margins on these goods can be substantially higher than margins on manufacturer branded goods. Table 3 illustrates the increased penetration of own-label packaged grocery items. As these levels rise, the power of the largest grocers rises, increasing their prospect of higher profits.

Table 3.1 *Own-label penetration in European packaged grocery (percentage of market)*

	1980	1990	1995
France	7	14	17
West Germany	5	14	20
Italy	5	6	8
Spain	2	6	7
UK	23	31	38

Source: Dobson & Waterson (1999)

There are unlikely to be any real substitutes for food retailers. So, in summary, we can see that the main determinants of competition in this industry relate to the intensity of rivalry, and the power that the large food retailers are able to exercise primarily over their suppliers and to some extent over their customers; new entrants may be constrained by the existence of planning and regulatory constraints plus the capital costs of entry. This may explain why Wal-Mart has acquired existing food retailers in Europe. Perhaps the biggest threat to the dominance of food retailers may lie in the advent of Internet shopping. A study by the Boston Consulting Group in the USA showed that online orders tripled in 1998 and the number of consumers buying online increased fourfold. The report also noted that 62 per cent of the on-line revenues in 1998 were from retailers who had businesses that predated the web. This is an issue to which we shall return in Chapter 7.

There is a different perspective to the power of retailers outlined in Illustration 3.2. Harvey (1999) argues that the nature of competition and innovation in UK supermarkets means that competition should be considered as between supply chains (especially supply, processing and distribution) as opposed to looking at the price of a shopping basket at a particular point in time. He argues that the 'shopping basket' is not an appropriate measure as it doesn't take into account the value that supermarket customers place on convenience, which is not priced into the overall equation. Supermarkets thus facilitate reductions or qualitative improvements in the uncosted time expended by the consumer in the equally economic essential activity of shopping. Harvey concludes that competition should not be judged in terms of the relationship between prices and costs at a point in time but rather in terms of the capacity to innovate over time leading to longer-term gains in quality, convenience and price.

In conclusion we re-emphasize that the market mechanisms and the ways in which they develop, which we have been discussing in this chapter, forms the crucial element in which products at what price are offered to customers.

4 The Legislative and Regulatory Framework

In Chapter 3 we reviewed the nature of the markets and the dynamics which control the manner in which markets react to competition. In this chapter we start by considering government-generated regulation introduced in the UK, USA and the European Union (EU) for the protection of consumers, with the intention of controlling the commercial and probably unfair 'free for all' that might result if there were no legislative framework. Given that in most Western countries the legislation exists, the question is whether it is directed at the most appropriate objectives? We then consider the influence and impact of legislation and regulations designed to preserve the environment.

4.1 Controlling Competition?

In the UK, the main provisions of the latest competition legislation, the Competition Act 1998, came into force on 1 March 2000. Up until that date the previous competition laws (including the Competition Act 1980, the Fair Trading Act 1973, and the Restrictive Trade Practices Act 1976) applied. EU competition legislation has been influential in forming the new legislation in the UK. Article 85 of the Treaty of Rome prohibits agreements which may affect trade between Member States and which have as their object or effect the prevention, restriction or distortion of competition within the Common Market, while Article 86 prohibits, 'abuse of a dominant position insofar as it may affect trade between Member States'.

By way of example we now briefly review some of the legislative organizations that have been created with the object of protecting the consumer.

Table 4.1 *The OFT's performance in 1998*

Area of Assessment	Target	Annual performance or number of cases	Performance against Target %
Consumer credit licensing	Issue licence within 20 working working days in 90% of cases.	20 912 licences issued	89
Credit reference disputes	Adjudicate within 2 months of receiving information from the parties.	44 cases	98
Estate agency	Adjudicate within 3 months of receiving final representations.	6 cases	100
Monopolies and anti-competitive practices	Ensure all parties are kept informed. Give substantive response to complaints and other correspondence within 30 days in 90% of cases.	1159 cases	95
	Complete an enquiry and decide on further action within six months in 75% of cases.	149 cases	81
Mergers	In confidential guidance cases, advise Secretary of State on likelihood of reference to CC within 19 working days of receiving satisfactory information in 90% of cases.	45 cases	56
	For mergers that have not been prenotified, to advise Secretary of State within 39 days in 90% of cases.	179 cases	81
Restrictive trade practices	To register agreements and assess significance of restrictions within 6 months of receipt of all information in 70% of cases.	763 cases	80
Responses to practices	Respond to enquiries from members of the public within 5 working days.	3736 enquiries processed	93
	Respond to student enquiries within 10 days.	376 processed	92
	Respond to business enquiries within 10 working days.	61 468	95

The Office of Fair Trading (OFT) – UK

The OFT's prime role is to protect consumers and encourage competition. The OFT is the government department responsible for promoting the economic welfare of consumers by enforcing UK competition policy.

The OFT maintains metrics of its performance against target under its Code of Practice on enforcement activities. The performance of most UK government-sponsored organizations is carefully monitored and the results are published. The areas of enforcement the OFT covers are: Consumer credit licensing; Credit reference disputes; Estate agency; Monopolies and anti-competitive practice; Mergers; Restrictive trade practices; Responses to enquiries. The results for 1998 are shown in Table 4.1.

As can be seen, the OFT records in great detail its performance against targets, and it makes the point that many enquiries, which are not timed, are dealt with directly over the phone. Overall our only criticism would relate to the time taken to deal with mergers, where, while recognizing that complex issues are likely to arise, time is likely to be of the essence for those involved.

The OFT is closely linked with the Competition Commission (CC) which is the body responsible for investigating matters that come under the 1998 Competition Act and related legislation. The CC had an annual expense budget in 1998/99 of £6.7m.

The CC published seven reports in 1998. It has no powers to initiate investigations. However, most requests for competition investigations come from the OFT and the CC has no choice as to which inquiries it undertakes. In 1998/99 the cost of maintaining the OFT and the CC was £30.8m (OFT – £24.1 m; CC – £6.7 m). We will now consider two examples of the working of the OFT and CC, first in relation to car sales in the UK and then in relation to the pricing of domestic appliances.

Motor car industry retail pricing in the UK.

The current motor car retail pricing structures have been in existence within the EU for more than ten years. The present *block exemption* rules were introduced to protect the EU motor industry from an influx of Japanese motor cars. However, these rules created a retail pricing structure that has worked against the British consumer.

In mid 1999 the Office of Fair Trading (OFT) at last took some action, citing the case of Volvo price fixing arrangements throughout the EU. The result overall, in the Volvo case, was that they were proved to be charging higher retail prices to UK consumers than customers elsewhere in the EU. More recently the CC investigated the conduct of car pricing relative to the rest of the markets in the EU. The UK government indicated that it will introduce legislation that will provide for punitive fines of up to three times a delinquent manufacturer's annual sales if a particular company is shown to have been manipulating European prices in this manner. This proposed fine is three times greater than the equivalent EU legislation.

Finally, the UK government thought the retail pricing structure of motor cars in the UK was probably not operating in a truly free market environment and thus was not in the public interest, and asked the CC to look into the situation. The first reviews of the Commission's report were made public, as may be seen in Illustration 4.1 below.

Illustration 4.1

Government Moves Towards Shake-up in New Car Sales

The government yesterday took the first step towards a fundamental shake-up in new car retailing, not just in Britain but across the whole European Union.

The Competition Commission report is likely to form the basis of a submission to Brussels on reforming the European block exemption on car prices.

Most consumer group and critics of the car industry regard the 14 year-old exemption set up to protect EU manufacturers from lean Japanese competitors as the main culprit in distorting new car prices.

They claim the exemption allows manufacturers to avoid normal competition law by supplying cars only through captive dealers, thereby fixing prices. Stephen Byers, the trade secretary, endorsed such allegations, and blew a hole in the industry view that the system protects consumer interests. 'It is clear that suppliers' current arrangements are not delivering cars to the private consumer at competitive prices,' he said.

Brussels often looks to Britain to lead on competition issues and the findings could spell the end of the exemption. But having blamed the *block exemption* for causing the problem, Mr Byers admitted he could not abandon it in the short term. The exemption is not due to expire until September 2002.

In spite of expectations that the Competition Commission could force an end to retailing practices, that means the franchise dealer system will remain in place. The DTI is studying ways to opt out of the exemption, but that could take at least a year to resolve.

Given that the real reason for inflated prices cannot be changed, the government was anxious that its proposals did not appear as second-best options.

Even so, there is no clear view on what sort of price cuts will arise from the commission's report, or whether it will change the way car makers do business. Many of the report's proposals will increase transparency in pricing, but that may not lead to significant reductions.

Source: Financial Times, 11 April 2000

So where does the UK consumer go from here? It seems that any significant change in retail car pricing will not happen until 2002. The rules of the game are complex and the professional body representing the consumer's interests should be fighting their case, but the UK National Consumer Council seems to have been silent on this issue. Surprisingly, nothing was really done about this until the first quarter of 2000, in spite of repeated consumer and newspaper protests about high motor car prices in the UK compared to retail prices in the remainder of the EU.

This point was reiterated in the European Commission report (1 May 1999) on car prices where it was shown that the UK remains the most expensive market for 62 of the 75 best selling models examined. Here, in our view, the case is reiterated of a controlled market situation activated by the manufacturers and the retailers.

It was, and is, certainly not a free market. It has taken a long time for the OFT and CC to take any action. Perhaps British consumers will soon achieve parity with their other European counterparts and enjoy the benefit of more competitive lower retail car pricing. At the time of writing the government did announce that some actions were underway as detailed in Illustration 4.2.

Illustration 4.2

UK Plans to Cut New Car Prices

The UK government on Monday published proposals aimed at cutting new car prices and opening up competition in the motor retail industry.

Stephen Byers, trade and industry secretary, said the draft order, following a damning Competition Commission report on UK car distribution, would lead to lower prices and increased sales.

The order, which will be subject to a 30-day consultation with the motor industry and consumer groups, will enable dealers to source cars from continental Europe, where pre-tax prices for some vehicles are up to 40 per cent lower than in Britain.

Mr. Byers said the government would also require suppliers to offer volume discounts to dealers who bought cars outright. They should be at similar levels to those offered to fleet buyers. Industry analysts calculate that the fleet buyers enjoy discounts of up to 30 per cent against list prices for new cars.

However, only the largest dealer groups are expected to take advantage of such a scheme. Most dealers stock cars on a sale or return basis.

'The market is not operating as competitively as it should,' said Mr. Byers. 'The measures that I plan to introduce should being about greater competition, and lower prices, by stopping suppliers discriminating against dealers.' But the government has decided not to embrace a call by the Competition Commission to consider Britain's unilateral withdrawal from the European block exemption on car sales.

The 14-year old exemption, due to expire in September 2002, allows manufacturers to distribute new cars only through captive dealers.

The department of trade and industry said it was discussing the future of the exemption with the European Commission. But it warned: 'It is expected to take at least a year to resolve.'

His intervention marks the culmination of a long-running consumer campaign for cheaper cars. The order is designed to implement the recommendations of a nine-month investigation into new car prices by the Competition Commission. The commission concluded that UK new car prices on average were 11 per cent higher than those in continental Europe and that carmakers were abusing their system of captive franchised dealers to operate an elaborate price-fixing cartel.

Industry executives claim that the fleet discount proposal, the most controversial element of the order, could prove unworkable.

They maintain that small dealers in country areas unable to buy in bulk would be forced out of business, to the detriment of consumers.

Manufactures also maintain that new car prices have already fallen by about ten per cent since April, when an outline of the intended order was published.

Mr. Byers acknowledged in a statement that car prices had fallen.

While welcoming the industry's response to the furore over car prices, Mr. Byers signalled that more needed to be done.

Following the consultation period, the order is expected to be signed in mid-July, implementing the remedies under the Fair Trading Act.

Source: Financial Times 13 June 2000

Another example of the way the CC works in the UK (or, my washing machine needs to be replaced)

Many of you will have had experience of deciding that the time has come to replace the washing machine. No doubt you have noticed that, whilst it's given good service over the past few years, it is now making a noise when running and really it now doesn't wash or spin-dry too well. You're fed up with all the poorly washed damp clothes hanging around the house and have decided you want a new machine. This is what is called in the business an impending 'distress purchase' – you've just got to get a new machine NOW.

You will recall from Chapter 2 that a washing machine is an appliance high in 'experience qualities', that is, attributes such as durability and ability to wash clothes properly can only be assessed and evaluated after purchase. This is still probably true even though the EU has tried to improve the consumer's ability to assess the performance of a washing machine by introducing a standard method of measuring the ability to wash under categories A to D.

So where do you go to buy the machine and how much homework or investigation do you carry out before doing so? Did you have a particular price and brand in mind?

Let's leave you suspended for a short time whilst we switch back to the OFT, in the UK. In 1995, the CC (MMC as it was then), was asked by the Director General of Fair Trading (DGFT) to investigate whether a monopoly situation existed in the UK in relation to the supply (other than by retail sale or hire) of washing machines. What this really meant was, did a market situation exist whereby if you went out to buy your new washing machine, you found that all the retailers large and small were offering the same machine at more or less the same price. Thus was the market in which you were trading truly competitive or were the products, quality and prices that you would pay, being manipulated in some way? The suggestion made by the OFT was that the price appeared to be fixed at a predetermined level and that a free competitive market did not exist.

So the CC was asked by the OFT to determine whether any company or person was engineering a market situation whereby prices were not solely being determined by market forces.

Let's go back to you now. You are out there simply trying to buy a washing machine. Would you buy the same make as before? The thoughts running through your head, would, we suggest include: Service matters – The manufacturer of my last machine called within 24 hours when a fault occurred. Should I simply go for the cheapest? Perhaps I could phone a manufacturer and ask what the price for his machines would be in the shops. I am concerned about look, colour and styling. Will it really wash clean? Does it have a matching Tumble Dryer? Will it fit in the kitchen? Does it really spin almost dry? You recall that even from new, the last one always left the clothes wet!

The CC reported in March 1998. Their investigation indicated that, at that time, the UK Domestic Electrical Appliance Industry was not operating as a freely competitive market. The CC concluded that by publishing Recommended Retail prices (RRPs), the manufacturers concerned were using these prices (together with incentives to certain retailers) as a tool to maintain a retail price level across a range of retail stores. Market analyses produced at the time and submitted to the CC showed otherwise. The CC report concluded that the use of RRPs for the selected appliances (washing machines, electric cookers, dishwashers and refrigerators) should be discontinued. The CC further decided that the practice of advertising RRP's should also be discontinued.

We analysed retail prices of domestic appliances and found that over the period May to December 1998 retail prices reduced by 1.3 per cent. By comparison in the two previous years the reductions were 2.3 per cent (1997) and 1.8 per cent (1996). Price trends in the industry reviewed over a six-year period 1993 to 1999 in the months of January to December indicate a similar rate of reduction. Thus the implementation of the report's recommendations made no impact on retail prices. We now question, in retrospect, whether the cost expended (by both the OFT/CC and the various companies involved) in undertaking the investigation was warranted.

Many potential purchasers are just not interested in going from shop to shop to assess prices. They are more likely to buy a personally known or recommended brand from an outlet that they trust, and then negotiate a deal in that store. They would have had some idea of prices from advertisements and – before the above legislation – from the selected manufacturer. Many now will use the Internet to benchmark prices. Are manufacturers in the UK going to be legally controlled as to whether they can advertise prices over the Internet? The Internet is a fast-moving and changing area of commerce. The OFT needs to look more closely at its methods of analysis as we move rapidly into the twenty-first century.

It is possible, in view of the 'value for money' initiatives now sponsored by the current government, that more attention would be given by the OFT before initiating such CC investigations, since much expense is incurred by all parties involved. The UK government subsequently announced (May 2000) that it was changing the structure of the OFT, with the creation of a new management board designed to beef up its defence of consumer interests. In view of our comments above we would support this move. The Secretary of State for Trade and Industry, said the new board, with a minimum of five members, would increase the OFT's transparency and accountability by broadening its influence and outlook. He went on, 'More board members will give a wider range of expertise to the organization, rather than executive power resting with one person. This will give businesses and consumers a stronger voice at the heart of the OFT'.

The European Union (EU)

Within the EU there are a large number of directives, concerned with competition policy already in place, together with a number of proposals under review. The commission deals with issues such as Antitrust, Liberalization, State Aid and international impact on the EU.

Each member state has national competition authorities and other related ministries. Typical examples of recent issues (May 2000) dealt with by the commission are shown in Table 4.2.

United States of America

In the USA there is the Federal Trade Commission (FTC) which enforces anti-trust and consumer protection laws, through its Bureau of Competition (BoC). The BoC aims to ensure that markets are competitive and it aims to eliminate all instances of unfair practice. Within the BoC is the Bureau of

Table 4.2   *Examples from the European Union*

Antitrust	Intervention against quota scheme to control public expenditure on pharmaceuticals
	Commences infringement proceedings against Glaxo Wellcome's double price system in Spain.
International	Clears Daimler-Benz/Chrysler merger.
	Approves UTA Telekom by VTOB and Swisscom.
	Clears acquisition by Arco of Unio Texas.
	Clears acquisition of Digital by Compaq.
State Aid	Sets national ceiling for coverage of regional aid.
Liberalization	Adopts Notice on the application of competition rules to Access agreements in the telecommunications sector.

Consumer Protection, which is divided into five divisions, each with its area of expertise covering Advertising practices, Enforcement, Financial practices, Marketing practices, Planning and Information, and Service Industry practices.

The US FTC has taken on some large and powerful organizations, such as AT&T and more recently Microsoft. In 1990 the FTC launched an investigation into Microsoft's alleged monopolistic practices. This investigation was closed in 1993, but taken up by the US Justice Department in the same year and was ended in 1994. In 1995 the Justice Department blocked Microsoft's purchase of Intuit and in 1997 it sued Microsoft accusing the company of violating the 1994 consent decree. In 1998 the Justice Department and 20 states filed suit against Microsoft alleging abuse of monopoly power. The trial started in October 1998 and in late 1999 the judge ruled that Microsoft 'engaged in a concerted series of actions' to suppress competition. In 2000 the judge ruled that Microsoft breached US anti-trust law and discussions were underway amidst the legal moves to arrive at a mediated settlement. Illustration 4.3 below sets out not only the position in the US, but also the knock-on effects for the EU.

Illustration 4.3

Ballmer Willing to Accept US Government Talks Offer

Steve Ballmer, chief executive of Microsoft, on Friday welcomed an offer from the US Justice Department for further settlement talks to help avoid a lengthy legal battle over the break-up of the world's biggest software company.

Mr. Ballmer, who is attending a European business summit organized by Belgium's employers' federation, told a news conference that Microsoft would 'still love the opportunity' to return to talks, although he refused to speculate on what the next steps might be.

Joel Klein, head of the Justice Department's antitrust division, had said the previous day that he was 'prepared to engage in meaningful settlement negotiations' to ensure that Microsoft did not repeat its monopoly abuses.

His comments echoed Judge Thomas Penfield Jackson, the trial judge who ordered Microsoft's break-up and a series of sweeping business restrictions on Wednesday.

Judge Jackson told the Washington post that he wanted both sides to 'swallow their own reluctance to compromise and reach a remedy that both sides, if not elated by, nevertheless are willing to, extend'.

Microsoft has already said it would be ready to negotiate. Bill Neukom, vice-president for law and corporate affairs, said the company would never 'close the door to good faith negotiations to resolve the differences'.

But the company had on Thursday dismissed Mr. Klein's comments as 'simply posturing'. Jim Cullinan, a Microsoft spokesman, said: 'If there was an opportunity for a serious discussion, we would be interested. But we don't believe that is what this is.'

There still seems to be little immediate chance that the two sides will negotiate an out-of-court settlement, after the collapse of exhaustive talks in April. Lawyers from both sides negotiated for three months without success, in spite of mediation by Richard Posner, head of the court of appeals in Chicago.

Microsoft's lawyers on Thursday filed for a stay of Judge Jackson's orders, including the strict curbs on its business practices which would come into force in just 90 days. The restrictions include requiring Microsoft to sell its Windows operating software on uniform terms to all computer makers, and disclosing its secret software code in a timely manner to the wider industry.

The company's break-up will be delayed until the appeals process is over, but its lawyers are keen to halt the judge's timetable preparing for break-up. Under the judge's final judgement, it has four months to detail plans for splitting itself in two.

The break-up order, if it is upheld on appeal, divides Microsoft into an operating system company managing Windows, and an applications company managing other products such as the Office package of business software.

Bill Gates, Microsoft's chairman and co-founder, accused the judge on Thursday of being prejudiced against the company. 'The judge apparently formed those opinions even before this case began,' he told CBS television. 'We had a previous case in front of this judge where the appeals court overruled him entirely.'

Mr. Gates insisted he was confident he would win on appeal, but admitted he was 'disappointed' with the judge's ruling. 'The rules were clear,' he said. 'Microsoft followed those rules, and now we simply need to get the higher court to make that clear.'

European Commission to continue inquiry

The European Commission on Thursday said it would look into whether the US ruling on Microsoft had implications for its own investigations into the company's dominant position.

'If Microsoft is ultimately to be broken up and the source code to Windows is disclosed, I imagine it will have some implications for our investigations, but it is too early to say,' said Amelia Torres, Commission spokeswoman. While the appeal process in the US was under way, the Commission would continue its investigations into Microsoft's market power, but the EU was still far from concluding its inquiries, she said.

Microsoft said the remedies of sanctions agreed with US regulators would be applied globally. That could remove the need for the

Commission to continue its investigations. But Tiffany Steckler, Microsoft spokeswoman, said, 'anything that is happening here in the Commission is completely unrelated to the US'.

The Commission has five inquiries under way into different aspects of the software giant's behaviour. Three of them relate to the company's dominance of the PC operating market based on complaints from competitors such as Sun Microsystems.

The Commission's latest inquiry was launched in February to look into Windows 2000, and whether the company had extended its dominance of PC operating systems into other markets for servers that connect PCs to the internet and ultimately, to electronic commerce.

Mario Monti, the EU's competition commissioner, said at the time: 'Whoever is dominant in server software is likely to control e-commerce too.' Microsoft responded to the inquiry by e-mail with reams of technical information that the Commission is still sifting.

The Commission is also looking at Microsoft's pricing policy for French software and investigating allegations that the company sold software more cheaply in Canada than in France. But Ms Torres said these investigations were still many months from fruition.

A more pressing priority for the EU is to examine Microsoft's plan to buy a stake in an UK cable company, Telewest. In March, Mr. Monti started a detailed four-month probe into Microsoft's £1.55bn ($4bn) deal to buy 29.9 per cent in Telewest, based on fears that the company could use its position to dominate the market for software used in television set-top boxes by cable companies.

The Commission is holding the second day of hearings in Brussels on Friday for the company and its rivals to put their cases and discuss the competition issues involved in the deal.

Source: Financial Times June 8 2000

Similar organizations exist in the other Western countries and it should be noted that similar government-sponsored organizations exist or are planned in most other countries. In Canada they have the Competition Bureau which is the government department responsible for overseeing the application and administration of the Competition Act. Most other developed countries have organizations similar to the Competition Commission in addition to the EU,

USA and Canada. This would include, Argentina, Australia, Brazil, Czech Republic, Japan, Korea, Mexico, New Zealand, Norway, Peru, Poland, Switzerland, Taiwan, Turkey, Venezuela.

4.2. The Environment, Health and Safety

Throughout the world over the past twenty-five years, people have become increasingly aware of the negative effect the actions of the human race have had on the environment in which we live. The preservation of our environment has become more of a public issue since the late 1970s and it has brought about significant changes in legislation throughout the world – aimed at preserving the world's environment to support life in the long term. We now will review some of the main issues.

The environment

Two of the most publicized environmental issues have been:

1. The generation of lead in the atmosphere from petrol-burning internal combustion engines with their generation of airborne lead compounds, which have been shown to have an adverse effect on health, particularly in children. This has now been controlled over the past few years following the introduction of lead-free petrol in most countries with the total withdrawal of leaded petrol within the EU in 2000.
2. The creation of 'greenhouse gases', Chlorofluorocarbons (CFC's), with their deleterious effect on the ozone layer.

The ozone layer lying in the outer layers of the earth's atmosphere forms a 'blanket' which reduces the intensity of the bursts of radiation from the Sun, for example, ultra-violet, which can cause skin cancers amongst other related maladies.

Action by governments throughout the world has already been taken on both issues, with the promotion of 'lead-free' petrol in most Western countries and the removal of CFCs from industrial and new domestic cooling processes, most particularly in refrigeration and air-conditioning equipment.

In fact most consumers have probably been unaware of the major changes that have taken place in the design and manufacture of the latter ranges of products, since these changes have been introduced, over the last five years, with little effect on prices and equipment performance. The UK government has published its challenges to industry which follows the agreements reached by the world's industrial nations in Kyoto, Japan in 1998. In particular the EU has agreed to target its member states to reduce greenhouse gases by 8 per cent by 2012 based on 1990 levels. The UK target is to reduce carbon dioxide emissions by 20 per cent by 2010 based on 1990 levels.

The challenge for the manufacturers and the cooling/refrigeration industry, as a whole, has been to achieve major changes in design and manufacturing techniques without any decrease in safety and without any overall cost increases.

Thus a major initiative has been launched world-wide to combat the threat of damage to the the ozone layer. Countries appear to be reacting to the threat with differing priorities. It does appear, for example, that the EU is accelerating its actions ahead of the USA. However much needs to done throughout the world if we are to slow the deterioration of the protection afforded us by ozone layers surrounding the Earth.

Recycling/recovery of waste electrical and electronic equipment.

Within the EU, Environmental, Health and Safety (EHS) directives are being proposed related to a range of issues including the control, recycling and recovery of waste electrical and electronic equipment. Typical products would include 'brown goods' (radio and TVs); 'white goods' (cookers, refrigerators, washing machines amd so on); computing and IT equipment; electronic toys and musical instruments. It is expected that, at the end of such products' life, procedures will be instituted to facilitate recovery and recycling. It is proposed that manufacturers will be responsible for organizing these processes. Thus consumers will normally be expected to return old appliances to their retailer when they buy a new one.

It will be evident that there will be a cost involved in meeting the requirements of the end-of-life recovery programme. At the present time the authorities in the UK envisage that the manufacturer will be responsible for the expense of operating the recovery programme. It is anticipated, naively we think, that the manufacturers will be able to recovery the cost from an increase in the initial sales price. Such products have a life of, say, ten years and we question how a manufacturer can reliably estimate the end-of-life product recovery cost ten years before the event. Since it is unlikely that consumers will pay more for products, the result, we believe, will be additional accountancy provisions in such companies' annual accounts, in order to provide for this contingent liability, with associated reduction in profits.

This potential legislation needs more considered thought by both government and industry.

Water conservation

The issue of water shortages throughout the world has come to the fore in the past few years and the importance of conserving water in apparently well provided areas, like parts of the UK and the USA, has become of increasing importance. Thus the recycling of 'used' domestic water, known as 'Grey Water' – all the waste-water produced in the home excluding foul water from the toilet, is being seriously considered. Up to a 30 per cent saving in domestic water consumption can be achieved by using Grey Water to flush toilets. Whilst some water authorities in the USA and the UK have expressed interest in this idea, no one has taken up the commercial challenge.

Finally, much attention is now being given to reduced water consumption in household and industrial appliances. For example, European-designed domestic washing machine water consumption is about one quarter of that of US-designed machines.

We believe more government attention, in all industrial countries, needs to be paid to ensure that appropriate action is taken in all areas of water conservation to preserve this vital source of life.

5 Supply Chain Management

In the face of today's fast moving industrial environment a business must have a strategy that sets out where it is going, and ahead of time, why and how it's going to get there. The overall strategy is dependent, amongst other things, upon the management culture which in many firms, large and small, varies in accordance with the changes in management thinking, which has been driven in great measure by the communications explosion over the past twenty years. Much of this has been influenced by US based management gurus like Peter Drucker, Michael Porter and Tom Peters. For example, back in 1982 Tom Peters and Bob Waterman were exhorting us, amongst other things, to: 'stay close to the customer'; 'be productive through people'; 'have a bias for action'. They talked about *excellent companies* and endorsed and celebrated the big manufacturing businesses like IBM and General Motors. Subsequently, Tom Peters (*Thriving on Chaos* 1987, and *Liberation Management* 1992) stated, at the same time as admitting that others had also pointedly suggested to him, 'that time had not treated some of *Search's* almost perfect instruments that well'. In 1992 his message was now to promote Organizational Structure and the speed at which things will be executed in the 'nanosecond nineties'. This was reinforced in 1999 when Bill Gates, the co-founder, chairman, and CEO of Microsoft, published a book entitled Business @ the Speed of Thought.

Thus Bill Gates, one of the most successful businessmen in the world, and Tom Peters along with many others are postulating that business in the twenty-first century will be enacted at speeds thought to be impossible only ten to fifteen years ago.

The adoption of the appropriate high level corporate strategy within a commercial enterprise in this fast-moving industrial environment will in many businesses require a change in management culture and organization.

There has always been discussion about which particular function or discipline drives or should drive the enterprise's strategy. In practical terms all the functions are interdependent. Such functions include Marketing, Research and Development (R&D), Sales, Finance and Supply Chain/ Manufacture. Whilst this chapter will concentrate on the manufacturing and supply chain, it is clearly impossible in a practical situation to look at this function in isolation from the rest. Furthermore, the relative power and influence of each function in an organization will often be very dependent on the background and strengths of the CEO and the senior team.

Since most companies are necessarily market-driven, it tends to be the marketing people who often emerge as the strategic drivers of a whole company. It is this team of people who creatively draw together and properly mix 'the corporate pot' of the enterprise's mission, objectives, competencies and attributes, at the same time as setting out for the other functions their own particular role in achieving the company's objectives and meeting the requirements of the strategy being developed. In some organizations one particular group's expertise may predominate, as for example, in a 'high tech' R&D-driven organization like a computer or telecommunications company, it is the products and technology group who would make a very influential contribution to the company's strategy.

However it is becoming more evident that the manufacturing process is assuming more importance in the 'corporate pot' and it is the object of this chapter to explore further this emerging trend within companies who manufacture products.

5.1 An Example of How One of the Best Companies Manages its Operations

One of the most outstanding companies in the world is General Electric (GE) with annual performance year on year outstripping previous years. An extract from the Chairman and CEO's statement for 1997 is shown in Illustration 5.1. Jack Welch stated that the total return on a share of GE stock was 51 per cent in 1997. This followed gains of 40 per cent in 1996 and 45 per cent in 1995. Jack Welch and his team must have 'stirred the corporate pot' somewhere near right over the previous three years – and indeed the fifteen or so years before that. GE's performance is indeed impressive.

Illustration 5.1

From the Chairman and CEO of GE, Jack Welch

An extract from the 1997 Annual Statement to Shareholders

In 1997, your Company had a great year – a record year.

- Ongoing revenues rose to $89.3 bn; up 13 per cent.
- Global (non-US) revenues rose to $38.5 bn; now 42 per cent of total revenues.
- Earnings increased to more than $8.2bn; up 13 per cent.
- Earnings per share increased 14 per cent to a record $2.50.
- Ongoing operating margin rose to a record 15.7 per cent, exceeding 15 per cent for the first time in the history of our Company.
- Operating cash flow rose to a record $9.3 bn. This, in combination with our Triple A debt rating, fuelled the investment of $17.2 bn in more than 75 industrial and financial service acquisitions in 1997.
- This record cash flow also allowed us to return $7bn to share owners: $3.5bn in dividends and $3.5bn for the repurchase of GE stock. Dividends were increased by 15 per cent, our 22nd consecutive annual dividend increase.
- In April, our share owners approved a two-for-one stock split, the fourth in the last 15 years.

We delivered these 1997 results by executing on our three major initiatives: globalization, a focus on product services and our drive for Six Sigma quality. Building on these same three initiatives will be critical to our future success. The uncertainty brought about by the Asian economic difficulties creates both challenges and opportunities. For GE, Asia represents about 9 per cent of our revenues (about half in Japan) – exposure that is by no means insignificant, but certainly manageable – and we are confident that we can minimize any impact on our existing operations.

It has been our repeated experience that business uncertainty is inevitably accompanied by opportunity. The Asian situation should be no exception; it should provide us with a unique opportunity to make the strategic moves that will increase our presence and our participation in what we know will be one of the world's great markets of the twenty-first century.

We've been down this path before. In the early 1980s, we experienced a United States mired in recession, hand wringing from the pundits and dirges being sung over American manufacturing. We didn't buy this dismal scenario; instead, we invested in both a widespread restructuring and in new businesses. We emerged into the recovery a much more competitive and productive company.

Globalization is one of the engines of GE growth, now and well into the next century. There will be dislocations and speed bumps on the road to prosperity in all the critical markets, but one cannot afford to write off any region in difficulty. Bad business management or bad government policies that weaken competitiveness can be remedied by tough restructuring and policy change. The same conditions that made restructuring and reform necessary frequently create a currency weakness that when coupled with increased competitiveness brought about by restructuring, leads the country out of recession, via internal growth and increased exports. *The path to greatness in Asia is irreversible, and GE will be there.*

GE delivered these results by executing on three major initiatives: globalization, focus on product services and a drive for Six Sigma quality. GE, over the fifteen years ended 1997, had, by sale and acquisition, successfully restructured its business by geographically shifting its supply chain (manufacturing and service bases) across North America, Europe and Mexico. In so doing they had developed a strategy that took account of and exploited the cyclic economic turbulence that characterized the economies of the world over that period − and which continues to do so today. Their determination to push further into Asia is evident in the CEO's statement.

The Six Sigma programme adopted by GE, Motorola, Allied Signal and others in the US, together with other similar quality initiatives, is argued to be one of the most powerful process improvement and change management tools available world-wide today. Historically many managers and directors have paid lip service to, for example, Total Quality Management (TQM), Business Excellence Management (BEM), Business Process Re-engineering (BPR) and similar initiatives with a notable lack of success. The issue is that if you cannot easily measure your progress, how can you set 'hard' targets for the management teams to achieve?

Most businesses, in the next two years, will have to move up a gear by changing their management culture in order to successfully compete in the fast moving 'e'–environment of today. Apart from the broadband network about to be offered to users by the telecommunications companies (Telcos), one of the critical success factors will be the manner in which a particular organization optimizes and measures its manufacturing performance and supply chain strategy. The establishment of such measures or metrics will, together with the Six Sigma or a similar quality improvement regime and coupled with a change in management culture, be the key enabling factor for success.

The adoption of a Six Sigma philosophy within a company demands a management trained in the Six Sigma methods and improvement processes, which are capable of delivering and leading the resulting change. Six Sigma probably represents one of the most demonstrably successful management and company change programmes available today and GE is now a world-leading exponent of this philosophy.

Illustration 5.2 suggests that the high growth expected in a 'high speed world' may to too optimistic at this time. But the issue now is whether the various companies and entrepreneurs will take up sufficient operating minutes on these networks soon enough for the telcos to recover the large investments that have been made by their shareholders.

Illustration 5.2

A High Speed World

More than 16 000 vans are out on the streets of the US, bringing a new communications industry to life. They are driven by AT&T engineers whose job it is to bring high speed internet services, house by house, office by office, to the masses. The same pattern is taking shape around the world, from Sweden – which last week announced plans to make the high speed internet available to every home in the country – to Taiwan where thousands of consumers have signed up for fast access from operators such as Gigamedia. In the UK, an auction of spectrum for 'third generation' high-speed mobile phones has just been so hotly contested that the government may raise £15bn ($23.7bn) – five times the original estimate.

> Broadband – the term applied loosely to any high-speed interactive communications service, whether it arrives through a cable TV connection, a wireless link or traditional telephone line – has become one of the great promises of the information revolution. It has become the focus of massive investment, drawing billions of dollars into companies that are building networks and creating services.
>
> *Source: Financial Times, 4 April 2000*

5.2 Key Factors in Formulating a Supply Chain Strategy

In the 'olden days', probably around twenty-five years ago, company managers and directors would sit down each year and contemplate how in the ensuing year they would fill up their factories (or factory) with work. In the seventies, in the UK, a large part of the consideration was dependent upon government-inspired changes in the economy. It was called 'fine-tuning', but it had the effect of completely disrupting the nation's economy over a period of about five years. It was better known as 'Stop Go'. Jim Collis, who was Director General of the Association of Manufacturers of Domestic Electrical Appliances, said in 1991, ' The whole area of what was called Stop Go, but which UK governments of the time called 'fine tuning', was responsible for making it impossible to plan'. He went on, 'I can recall when I was Managing Director of a consumer electronics company, we used to sit around a table, on budget days, listening to the Chancellor (of the Exchequer) and at the end of his speech we would be faced with either closing a factory or trying to work out how to double our production'. (Wolfe, 1996.) The communications and computer power explosion had not yet arrived to the world's industries.

Today we just could not live in a 'seventies UK industrial environment'. Our world is global not national. We want to get high quality raw materials, components and finished product in the right quantities, to our factories on time or rather Just-in-Time. Our manufacturing and more accurately supply chain horizons stretch all round the world and we do not view supply from our own or localized manufacturing sources as a given, in any raw material, sub-assembly or product supply scenario. Our industrial and political leaders have to view the world as their source of supply which will be based on close long-term commercial agreements with factories based upon stable political relationships with such countries. Such suppliers were often previously seen as low quality, opportunistic and tactical sources of supply.

This is not the case today where these previously embryonic manufacturing organizations have become strategic sources of supply. This new and exciting trading opportunity has been enabled by the ability that we now have to send complex video, data and voice communications accurately in minutes around the world. This, together with our growing capability and the ease with which we can rapidly travel and ship goods to and from previously remote locations, together with the desire and newly acquired capability of this type of supplier, has created trade that has become profitable to both parties. Moreover, based on a stable political relationship with such suppliers, the supply paradigm has changed as regards the whole approach to the procurement of raw materials, piece parts and sub-assemblies. Particular world industries like telecommunications, computers and automotive have found that in order to remain competitive (design and cost) and deliver manufactured product on time, vertically organized manufacture in-house does not maximize margins. Ford, for example, are pursuing profits right down the value chain of the car industry. Following the lead taken by General Motors, Ford is trying to get its suppliers to subassemble more of its cars and may even subcontract final assembly. However this way of working requires that a firm business plan is pre-established. In this world of long supply lines one cannot operate in a 'seat of pants' industrial environment of short-term government or management style. To attempt to do otherwise will mean that supplies will not arrive and manufacturing programmes will be thrown into confusion – not to mention the unsatisfied customers (internal and external) who will not get their deliveries on time. Thus we have get our plans and strategy right and much depends on top management's ability to deliver the strategic plan.

Illustration 5.3

Supply Chain Management at Marconi

Marconi Communications, a wholly owned subsidiary of Marconi Plc, has more than tripled its annual sales of telecommunications products to approximately £3bn over the period July 1998 to 31 March 2000. The original UK company had two large UK telecommunications equipment manufacturing units based in Liverpool and Coventry. The key manufacturing processes are: production of multilayer Printed Circuit Boards (PCB's) where the boards provide the complex interconnects for the high component density integrated circuits mounted on the PCB's: see Figures 5.1 and 5.2. The so-called 'stuffing' (with electronic chips) of the boards is performed by specialist automated machinery which facilitates the employment of a small number of skilled technicians who can maintain and operate the machines. The initial assembly work is now sufficiently deskilled that it can be outsourced to specialist subcontractors – sub-assembly factories #1, 2, 3 and so on. The final assembly of the PCB's into boxes, followed by configuration (tailoring the final unit to meet a customer's specific requirements) and testing is done in 'Product Assembly and Customisation Centres' PACCs #1. 2, 3 and so on. The testing phase is performed by suitably programmed (software controlled) automatic test machines, supervised by the skilled operators. The 'know-how' contained in the configuration phase represents the key intellectual property owned by the company. The whole operation has to be carried out to world-class quality standards.

In 1998, the PCB's were manufactured in the company's UK based factories in Coventry or Liverpool or subcontracted to UK companies, whilst the remainder of the manufacturing, assembly and test processes were carried out in-house.

The expanded company now has its own manufacturing facilities in the UK, Italy, USA, Germany, South Africa and China – eight factories in all. The challenge and opportunity has been to optimize the company's expertise and facilities by analysing the company's capabilities and the processes, in order to produce a quality product in the volumes required in most countries of the world.

Marconi has decided that the manufacturing process splits primarily into subcontractors capable of supplying PCB's to those manufactur-ing units where the assembly, configuration and final test is done. Thus the high-level process configuration is as shown in Figure 5.1. The key to this is the centralized planning hub which coordinates the whole operation.

The challenge to the Supply Chain operation is enormous and this is the key to the company's success.

Whilst the people and physical organization are mission-critical, the whole operation is dependent upon the availability of world-class

IT systems capable of maintaining world-wide communications 24 hours per day, seven days each week, 365 days per year.

The company, like many other large industrial organizations, has ERP (Enterprise Resource Planning) systems throughout the group. The emergence of these complex and business-critical systems has spawned a sector of the management consulting industry with 'claimed expertise' in ERP systems. Any company contemplating installing such a system must be extremely selective about the choice of advisers and bear in mind that the exercise will be complex involving a great deal of investment and culture change and will take years to completely install. It is our experience that the area that causes most difficulty is the people and their reluctance to change the way they work when operating in a new ERP environment.

We have much to learn about this new fully automated world and people with their appropriate training and experience are still needed to operate these very sophisticated systems and processes. More thought needs to be given to the education of people to meet this challenge.

Reproduced by permission of Marconi plc.

The prime issue that must be addressed concerns the location of manufacturing units. Is the chosen location compatible with 'supply chain' and 'routes to market' plans? In the past a business would have preferred, in principle, to locate factories as near to its markets as possible. However, the trend over the past few years, most particularly in Europe and the USA, has been to 'outsource', that is to move the low added value activities 'off-shore' to lower cost and developing regions such as Turkey (from Western Europe), Mexico (from the USA) and China (from USA and Europe).

The resulting supply chain model at Marconi Communications is shown in Figures 5.1 and 5.2. The order entry location is in the same region as the sales/commercial offices. This information is sent to regional planning centres located across the world. The order fulfilment activity is placed in a number of world-wide manufacturing hubs whose output feeds the customers.

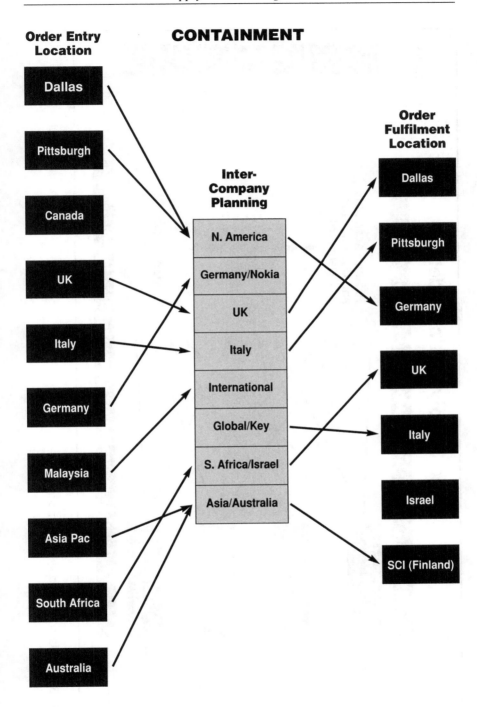

Figure 5.1 *Order fulfilment at Marconi*

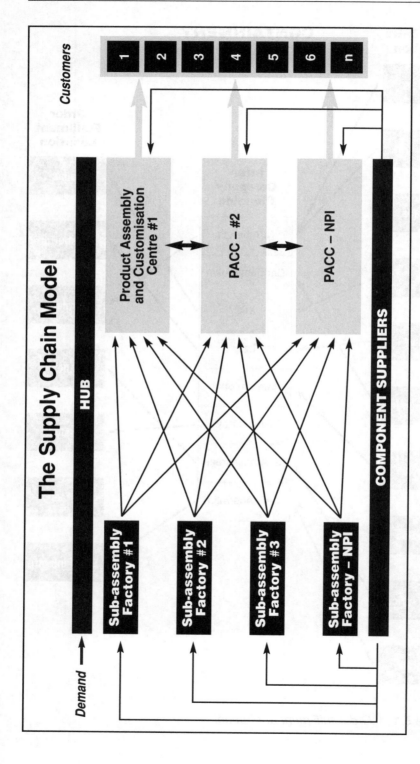

Figure 5.2 *Marconi's supply chain model*

In considering this supply chain, many parts and sub-assemblies are coming from the developing countries. Thus logistics is becoming one of the key competencies that companies in the developed countries have had to develop in fostering their supply chains. In seeking to develop reliable and efficient supply chains, the leading companies of the world will have to ensure that their approach to creating new sources of supply to ensure sustainable competitive advantage is sufficiently long term as opposed to creating a short term cost-cutting exercise.

We have mentioned some of the effects of globalization in Chapter 1. In considering supply chain management two issues come to mind. First, companies placing low added-value work in these locations often create, in the longer term, an overseas competitor, with in many cases a potentially large home market, who has now learnt to build and develop the product on his own. Thus this practice of outsourcing has to be treated with some caution by the outsourcer but in our opinion the end product designer and supplier has no choice but to keep innovating or become a good 'has been' in its market. Probably one of the biggest threats to the global telecommunications industry is the growth of Chinese manufactured telecommunications equipment. Most of the 'high-tech' factories in China were started in joint ventures together with some of the leading Western manufacturers – for example Siemens, Nortel, Marconi and so on. The Chinese insisted that the businesses were started employing the latest technology and with long-term technology licensing agreements. Thus the majority of these new Chinese companies are totally up-to-date and continue to grow and develop their skills with the support of leading Western companies. Many people in the West comment that these factories will never be a threat outside China since the Chinese have not yet learnt the art of achieving repetitive quality and exporting to the West. We are convinced it is only a question of time before the Chinese fully realize their potential and start to develop expertise in selling in Western markets. In fact, in a recent survey of Hong Kong (Financial Times 27 June 2000) Hong Kong's continuing role of exporting goods manufactured in mainland China was questioned, as more foreign companies attempt to bypass the territory and deal directly with the increasingly market-orientated mainland.

Second, doubts have been expressed as to whether globalization is a good thing. We would argue that it is a phenomenon that is affecting us all, and one which all firms need to take account of in developing their overall strategy and within that the management of their supply chain. Illustration 5.4 is a timely reminder and a warning to the proponents of globalization.

Illustration 5.4

Storm over Globalisation

Breaking down barriers is controversial work. That will be clear on 30 November, when as many as 100,000 demonstrators will march through Seattle, ostensibly to protest at the launch, at the World Trade Organisation (WTO) summit, of a new round of trade liberalising talks. But their real target is globalisation, broadly defined...

Around the world, support for free trade is weak at best; and the WTO is 'copping the blame' for the perceived evils of globalisation. It is under attack from trade unions, greens and even consumer groups, all of whom say its rules advance big companies' global ambitions at the expense of jobs and the environment. They also attack the WTO for being secretive and unaccountable. Such arguments will gain ground unless the case for globalisation is made with renewed vigour.

Source: The Economist, 27 November 1999

5.3 Managing Supply Chains in Service Industries

We have discussed an electronic equipment manufacturer's view of managing the global manufacturing challenge, but at the other end of business, retailers are the closest to the ultimate customer and are pushing hard to grow their business in the global economy. Like manufacturers, they are trying to maximize profitability but they have to give much consideration to the costs of providing service, often by forming alliances with former competitors.

An extremely important area of the retail service industry is the banking sector. Many consumers, and even the banking industry itself, have tended in the past to forget that even when finance is in short supply, the banks' job is still to provide a financial service. More open competition and the advent of fast reliable communication has forced individual banks to improve their total quality of service to customers whilst, at the same time, reducing operating costs. Thus banks right across Europe are overhauling their customer-facing services by employing the new technologies together with facility consolidation, in order to create more efficiency within their internal operations or 'back offices'. These operation centres are effectively the engine rooms feeding the key interfaces with their customers. This view was echoed in the extract from the Financial Times shown in Illustration 5.5.

Illustration 5.5

The Focus of Attention in the Frontline

The back office has traditionally been the least noticed cog in a bank's machine. But while there may be little glamour in the business of processing retail products such as current accounts, deposit accounts and mortgages, the back office has recently become the focus of frontline attention. Across Europe banks have been making use of new technology to overhaul back-office operations by bringing processing out of their branches and into centralised units. For example, Lloyds TSB, the UK bank, announced an efficiency drive last February which involved the loss of 3000 jobs, stemming mainly from the centralisation of computer operations and consolidation of large scale processing operations, including the complete removal of all back-office processing from branches. The bank pointed out that as a result of changes, it should be able to reduce its cost-to-income ratio to 35 per cent by 2002 – easily outstripping its nearest rivals.

The main German banks, Deutsche Bank, Dresdener Bank, Commerzbank and HypoVereinsbank, are also under pressure to increase the efficiency of their back offices, given the traditional high cost of retail banking in the country.

Indeed, merging back offices was one of the stated reasons behind the proposed merger of Deutsche and Dresdener, and the collapse of the deal has put renewed pressure on both banks.

Source: The Financial Times, 26 May 2000

Thus banks, as others in the retail sector, have to change the way they work by re-engineering themselves. A new breed of e-based bank is emerging that does not offer the provision of current accounts, along with all the expenses they involve, and they are targeting the more profitable areas of the industry – credit cards, consumer loans, savings accounts and the like.

Thus the perceived and realized gains from globalization and supply chain management vary from industry to industry and one has to take care in extrapolating experience from one trade sector into another.

Overall the message is clear. As a result of many factors the world is becoming much smaller from a business standpoint. A consumer in any country will be bombarded by product and sales propositions based on product supply strategies that may emanate from overseas. Much confusion may result which could cloud the proposition being offered. However, the consumer may benefit from the improved quality of product or service coupled with lower priced propositions. We are entering a time where the total 'value for money' opportunities offered to consumers will prove to be better than ever before.

6 Markets in Action

This chapter considers a number of examples of markets. A range of examples and issues are considered so that we can lay the groundwork for a consideration of what the future may hold in our final chapter. We start by revisiting the PC market which we discussed first in Chapter 3. We then look at the international air travel industry, a subset of the tele-communications industry, and the car industry. We conclude the chapter by reconsidering retailing. We consider this to be an important dimension in our understanding of competition, because the way that organizations relate to each other across the value chain, as well as how consumers conceive of purchasing goods (usually from retail outlets or their equivalent), will determine whether or not a reasonable profit is earned from the sum of the value activities. It will also determine whether a reasonable deal is provided for the consumer.

6.1 The Personal Computer Market

We first considered the PC market in Chapter 3. We noted then that suppliers to PC manufacturers, namely Intel, had concerns about the power of the retailer in the UK market. We will now consider in more detail the development of the PC market based on Illustration 6.1 overleaf.

Illustration 6.1

A Bad Business

For the past 15 years the personal-computer industry has walked tall. But now it is hobbling.

Most of the geeks shoving their way into New York's Javits convention centre for last week's PC Expo. saw only the usual cornucopia of computing delight. As always, the message of the PC industry's annual extravaganza was that everything is getting smarter, faster, cheaper. Never has the strength of Moore's Law – that computing power will double every 18 months – seemed to be more gloriously affirmed.

Those prepared to look harder might, however, have seen the writing on the wall for PC makers. Though they will sell more machines in the next few years, 1999 may prove the high-water mark for revenues in the industry's American heartland. As for profits, even in today's market they are hard to come by – witness recent losses at Compaq, the word's biggest PC maker.

Although some of the Compaq's difficulties are unique, stemming from its acquisition of Digital in 1998, few of its competitors are thriving either. Both IBM and Hewlett-Packard have struggled to make money from PCs. Even Dell, the acknowledged pace-setter, has found its margins under pressure since it began to sell cheap PCs for the first time earlier this year. As for most of the rest, don't ask.

These low profits partly reflect over capacity and competition for market share. But PC makers are also worried that the relentless cycle of upgrades, stroked by marketing and technology, is losing steam. The main cause is the Internet, the very phenomenon that many believed would be their greatest opportunity. Now, some Internet service providers (ISPs), such as America Online, are even giving PCs away.

The shock is all the greater because the past 12 months have been exceptional. Demand from businesses has been driven by the need to replace older PCs that were vulnerable to the millennium bug. In the consumer market, the Internet bandwagon is driving all before it, with first-time buyers, now the main engine of sales growth, accounting for

27 per cent of all unit sales, according to Forrester Research, a high-tech consultancy. At the same time, more households that already have one machine will buy another to ease the competition for mouse-time between family members. Forrester predicts that this year American consumers will buy 16.9m new PCs – 17 per cent more than last year – raising household penetration to 52 per cent.

However, both business users and consumers are increasingly happy to buy cheap 'good enough' PCs without the latest, fastest and most expensive chips from Intel. Despite raging demand, average prices of both business and consumer PCs will tumble by about 14 per cent this year. As a result, total revenues will be only 2–3 per cent higher than in 1998.

That is an awful omen for next year. Few businesses will be replacing the more-than-adequate machines they have just bought. And the recent flood of consumer buyers will subside. The remaining first-timers are likely to be more resistant to the complexity and expense of PCs, and to the cost of using the Internet. Meanwhile, supply will overflow. Having ramped up production over the past couple of years, Intel and its low-price competitors such as AMD will not be able to scale it back at multibillion dollar chip plants, and will swamp the market, cutting chip prices even faster.

Forrester reckons that next year's PC-industry revenues in America could be as much as $8bn – or 14 per cent – lower than they were in 1999. There may be little recovery in later years, because falling prices will offset modestly growing sales. IDC, another forecaster, thinks that the average price of PCs will fall less dramatically than Forrester expects. Even so, it too reckons the value of business and home desktop PC sales will be no higher in 2003 than it is today.

The PC market has seen boom and bust before. The difference this time is the absence of what was the main impetus for PC sales in the past: the need for frequent upgrades to run the ever more sophisticated products of the software industry.

Users have little reason to change the PCs they have bought over the past year. The latest release of Microsoft's Office, a suite that includes such programs as Word, Excel and PowerPoint, demonstrates that software developers cannot think of any useful new features that require more than the computing power of current machines. Games run better and more reliably on dedicated consoles such as PlayStation and Nintendo. Sony's PlayStation 2, to be launched next year, will even rival the consumer PC by adding a web-browser, email and a digital video-disc-drive, which, among other things, will enhance the machine's storage capacity.

But the real rebel against the tyranny that says PC owners must always upgrade is the Internet itself. Very little web content will require PC owners to buy new hardware; every new website will prolong the life of existing hardware. Websites depend on attracting as many visitors as they can. Nobody would want to limit the appeal of their sites by designing them to work properly only on the fastest PCs.

If users have spare money to devote to computing, they are more likely to spend it on increasing the bandwidth of their connection or on staying online for longer, both of which will benefit ISPs and cable operators rather than the PC industry. Although Dell says that people typically upgrade their PCs six months after getting a broadband connection, even today's cheaper PCs can cope with the fastest cable modems. Forrester's Eric Schmitt says that users are likely to spend whatever money they have left over on something that makes a difference, such as a snazzy flat-panel screen or a rewritable CD-ROM drive.

By the time firms get around to replacing the PCs they have bought in the past 12 months, corporate computing will have been trans-formed. As firms rush to become e-businesses, client/server computing, which put the PC at its core, is giving way to Internet computing, in which applications and data run entirely on servers. When little is asked of the PC other than to gain access to these servers by means of a browser, users will not be able to spot much difference between old PCs and new ones.

What does all this mean for the PC industry? In a single word, pain. Internet computing will lead to lots of portable 'thin clients' that will be inexpensive alternatives to laptops. Desktop PCs will remain competitive, but only because of their amazing cheapness. Less mature markets in Europe and Asia will absorb some of the over capacity, but not for long. The same market dynamics apply there too: after all, the Internet is nothing if not global.

So the PC firms will have to learn new tricks to survive. Apple's success with the novel design of its iMac shows one way to go. Super-efficient direct sellers such as Dell and Gateway are starting to sell other electronic devices and are even determined to become ISPs themselves. Last week Michael Dell, Dell's founder, said that he means to start his own service. Gateway, for its part, is in talks to buy EarthLink, a rival of America Online. Meanwhile, technology heavyweights such as IBM and Hewlett-Packard might question whether they should stay in such a commodity business at all. IBM already makes more money selling its technology to firms like Dell than it does flogging its own PCs.

Wintel's worries

For Microsoft and Intel, the two halves of the Wintel monopoly, life also seems likely to grow harder. The $50 that Microsoft extracts for each copy of the Windows operating system will look increasingly egregious. With the Justice Department watching, Microsoft will be wary of exploiting its monopoly to the full. Commercial versions of Linux, an increasingly popular alternative operating system, also give PC makers a stick with which to beat Microsoft – if they feel brave. As for Intel, it must now realise that merely accelerating its product introductions is not working. Intel will doubtless pack a lot of its chips into new Internet devices, so long as it prices them cheaply. But it is vital for the Wintel pair's margins that firms rush to buy servers running Microsoft's industrial-strength, but delayed, Windows 2000 and Intel's equally late 64-bit successor to the Pentium.

And what of the market leader? Poor Compaq falls halfway between an IBM that sells technology and services and a Dell that is a slick build-to-order assembler, a condition that selling its AltaVista search engine has done little to remedy. The firm's chairman and acting chief executive, Ben Rosen, may even feel that he did Eckhard Pfeiffer a favour when he sacked him in April.

Source: The Economist, 3 July 1999

Given the competition for market share and overcapacity in the industry there are unlikely to be any new manufacturers of PCs. So we would not expect to see any new entrants into the marketplace, though this may not preclude the development of new 'brands' for PCs being available to customers. Such brands may be retail brands. The rivalry between manufacturers is intense, driven primarily by the nature of the industry. More importantly, the battle for market share, which historically has been driven by upgrades developed by suppliers, is changing. Moore's Law, which fuelled the expansion of the industry historically, was based on developments in microchips largely produced by Intel, and software developments driven by Microsoft. If this article is correct these twin drivers are no longer as relevant to the future development of the industry as they were in the past. The illustration argues that although volumes will increase, prices would decline for both business and consumer PCs. Although the market for PCs that the article considers is North America, Europe and other parts of the world are not that far behind. Given the high-level penetration in consumer markets in the US and given that most firms will have equipped themselves to deal with the year 2000 bug, PC manufacturers' ability to grow revenues and profits is going to be constrained.

What may be happening here is a fundamental shift in the nature of the industry, driven largely by substitute products. You may recall that we defined substitutes as those products or services that provide the consumer with the same output or service as that of the industry itself. The fact that the potential of substitutes has now come to the fore is a function of changes largely outside the industry, that is the development of the Internet. This has focused attention on smaller and cheaper Internet boxes, a concern for bandwidth (the size of the 'pipe' connecting the box to the Internet), and the developments of other related technologies such as PlayStation's which can also access the Internet. Why would a consumer, for example, who seeks to use the Internet for entertainment, home shopping, e-mail services and so on, need an extremely powerful (in technical terms anyway) PC when one of their primary uses is connectivity to the Internet? As the article points out, this also has important consequential effects for those major and powerful suppliers to the PC manufacturers, Intel and Microsoft. For businesses, which as we shall see later need to develop capabilities in e-commerce, the development will focus on running applications and data on servers with a decline in the importance of the PC. As we noted in Chapter 3, most businesses' PC acquisitions are now on a replacement cycle, and as the article itself points out, lower power PCs can cope with new developments given the shift to a server-based system.

PC manufacturers themselves clearly take these changes seriously as their links with Internet Service Providers demonstrates. The benefits to consumers will only be determined by more complex features which we shall discuss later when we consider the changes in retailing. While better products (in terms of functionality, technical specifications, reliability) may well become available in the future, the prices which will be charged will be a function of the relationship between the manufacturer, their supplier and their distribution network. This is an issue which we shall consider in more depth when we look at the development of retailing in the final section of this chapter.

6.2 International Air Travel

Illustration 6.2 sets out some of the issues confronting the development of international airlines. In considering these, the first point of note is that the nature of the service is quite different from PCs, for example. A seat on an aircraft is in effect a very perishable item. If an aircraft takes off with an empty seat the revenue foregone cannot be reclaimed on the next flight or the next day. Unlike most goods, where if we do not sell the PC on the one day then we may be able to sell it on the next, once an aircraft has taken off without the revenue from the empty seat, that revenue has gone forever. The same applies to most services such as hotels and professional services. Another feature of the airline business, which is also shared by many other similar service businesses, is highly fixed costs. The costs involved in operating aircraft are inherently independent of the number of passengers carried. As a consequence of the perishability of the 'product' and the relatively high fixed costs, the industry has developed a range of techniques designed to fill aircraft seats. These range from cheap fares in economy class and special deals for holiday companies, to very sophisticated management information systems designed to manage the overall yield on both individual aircraft and on the fleet as a whole.

Illustration 6.2

Flying in Circles

Airlines are coalescing into three or four alliances. But the industry is still unstable and confused.

You are booked on the cheapest business flight from London to Seoul. You are going via Paris to pick up an Air France direct flight. On the way to Heathrow you discover that the flight from Paris is actually operated by its alliance partner, Korean Airlines, though the flight code said 'AF'. Instead of travelling with the airline you chose, you are about to board a plane with a carrier whose safety record has been sullied by crashes and near misses. Welcome to code sharing, the practice that shapes the route networks of most of the world's 500 airline alliances.

Air France and several other international airlines recently decided to suspend their code sharing with the Korean carrier, on account of its poor safety record. Yet, despite the dangers of putting your brand in someone else's hands, alliances have grown tenfold in the 1990s, as airlines seek to sell tickets to a wider range of destinations without actually flying to more. Partners in an alliance sell each other's flights and even book blocks of seats on each other's aircraft. By combining networks, airlines can feed extra traffic on to their trunk routes and reap economies of scale.

Bilateral alliances once used to be notoriously unstable, but, until recently, they had seemed to be settling down. A study by the Boston Consulting Group (BCG) found that two-thirds of alliances today have lasted more than three years. In 1992–95 two-thirds fell apart. Moreover, three or four super-alliances have gradually been emerging, which between them account for about two-thirds of air travel (see Table).

Hubs and spokes
Share of world traffic, 1998

	Per cent
Oneworld	
American Airlines, British Airways, Canadian airlines, Cathay Pacific, Quantas, Iberia, Finnair, Lan Chile	18
Star	
United Airlines, Lufthansa, SAS, Thai Airways, Air Canada, Varig, ANZ	16
Delta	
Delta Airlines, Air France, Austrian Airlines, Swissair, Sabena	12
KLM/NW	
KLM, Northwest Airlines, Alitalia, Continental Airlines, America West Airlines	11
Others	43

For years the industry expected most of the 200-odd international airlines eventually to consolidate into four or five mega-carriers. But bans on foreign ownership and lingering government control over routes and flights preclude international mergers and limit airlines' entry to new markets. In effect, these super alliances are coming as close to actual mergers as aviation's Byzantine regulations allow.

However, these four emerging groups now face another wave of instability. The cause is a decision last month by Air France, one of the last big unaligned airlines, to join a group led by America's Delta AirLines. According to BCG's John Lindquist, 'it may even have postponed for a time the end-game that seemed to be approaching'.

Immediately after Air France's decision to join Delta, SAir (the parent group of Swissair) decided to sell its 4 per cent equity share in Delta and sign a bilateral code-sharing deal with rival American Airlines (AA). If Swissair (and its European sidekicks, Sabena and Austrian) sever all their links with Delta and Air France, the Franco-American team will have to build an entirely new alliance. Equally, the Oneworld alliance between AA, British Airways (BA) and others looks shakier following the American airline's deal with Swissair's boss, Jeff Katz (a former AA pilot). AA's commitment to Oneworld may be wavering: henceforth AA could have two European hubs: crowded Heathrow (through BA) and Brussels (through Swissair/Sabena). According to Keith McMullan of Aviation Economics, a London consultancy, BA's best response might be to bring Swissair into the Oneworld group, especially as both airlines concentrate on business customers.

What's in it for me?

Alliances purport to offer passengers seamless travel, with better connections, more airport lounges and frequent-flier benefits wherever they go, provided they stay within the alliance. Given that alliances sometimes limit passengers' choice by combining their marketing and even jointly managing capacity on some routes, you might expect reduced competition to lead to higher fares.

Yet airlines insist that alliances actually reduce ticket prices, and their claims are backed up by recent evidence. David Marchik, of America's department of transportation, points out that since 1996 fares have dropped by 17 per cent between America and the

European countries with which it has 'open skies' deals that scrap flight restrictions. These deals mostly coincide with routes flown by alliances, such as those between Lufthansa and United Airlines or North-west and KLM.

The idea that alliances are at least partly to thank for these cheaper fares is supported by a study last winter by Jan K. Brueckner and W. Tom Whalen of the University of Illinois. They found that fares for transatlantic journeys involving several legs are 18–28 per cent cheaper if done within the route networks of allied airlines rather than through non-aligned carriers. The reason for this, they say, is that alliance partners gain by practising 'cooperative pricing' whereby they seek to maximise the benefit to all the members. This leads to a lower fare for the whole journey. An airline that is not part of an alliance inevitably tries to milk its one leg of the ticket journey for as much money as it can.

Change from within

Despite the continuing instability, the alliances are thinking about how they can boost their revenues by moving beyond joint marketing. At the moment, 70 per cent of alliances have code-sharing and 50 per cent have frequent-flier programmes, but only 15 per cent, according to the BCG report, try and save costs by sharing such facilities as catering, training, maintenance and aircraft-buying. As alliances begin to pool these activities, they will re-shape the airline industry from within.

At the moment there are two extremes. BA is outsourcing as much as it can, turning itself into a virtual airline that concentrates on running flights and marketing – where it has quite enough on its plate. (Not only does the airline already face an antitrust investigation in America, but on July 14th the European Union fined it E6.8m – $6.9m – for paying travel agents to create a barrier against other airlines. BA is appealing against the fine.) Specialisation creates scope for consolidation among companies that provide BA with the services it will buy in. Enter the airlines at the other extreme, notably Swissair and Lufthansa, which want to make money from services as well as flights.

Consider again the Swiss response to Delta's French connection. Whereas most alliances now no longer involve equity stakes, SAir is buying stakes in several airlines. With the proceeds of its Delta sale it bought 20 per cent of South African Airways; it also has stakes in five smaller European carriers, including Portugal's TAP and Portugalia and France's AOM.

SAir uses these partnerships to sell airline services. It probably makes more money from its interests in airline catering (in which it owns 20 per cent of the world market), ground handling, maintenance and air cargo than it does from actually flying. On July 13th SAir bought another ground-handling business, Dynair, from Alpha Airports for $155m. SAir wants to use its equity stakes and its alliances to supply such services to its partners, and to build itself a global position at the unglamorous end of the airline business, making sure that the meals are there, that the luggage is loaded and that there is no empty space in the below-decks cargo hold.

Most airline services command only thin margins (catering is one example), but a company that provides them across the world can achieve economies of scale. SAir's strategy is not unique. Lufthansa is doing something similar, by using its partners in the Star alliance as a market. The Lufthansa group includes the world's largest maintenance company, the largest airline caterer (with 29 per cent of the market), the leading air-cargo operator and a big systems company. For BCG's Mr Lindquist, one of industry's most revealing recent events was when the Star Alliance obliged Scandinavian Airlines Systems (SAS) to drop SAir's Gate Gourmet in favour of LSG Skychef, which is part of its German rival, Lufthansa.

However they go about growing together, the super alliances have formidable challenges ahead. Are their members selling their own brand or the brand of the alliance? Ask most airlines and they lamely say 'both'.

But these alliances will become real mergers only if the liberalisation of international aviation goes much further. America has signed 33 open-skies deals around the world, which free airlines to fly where and when they want without government interference. Until open skies are universal and limits on freight ownership are relaxed, airlines will continue to live in the twilight world of shifting alliances rather than the clear day of global consolidation.

Source: The Economist, 19 June 1999

As we examine the airline industry there are two issues which appear to have a major impact on competition. The first is the nature of the industry that we referred to earlier. As the article notes, airlines always try to reap scale economies either by combining routes or by combining services (such as catering and maintenance). Parts of the industry are very competitive. Some of the routes, for example the transatlantic routes between Europe and the US, have a number of carriers and overcapacity. In order to deal with this competitive situation airlines appear to be adopting three different strategies. Some, like BA, outsource as much as they can and concentrate on flying planes and marketing. Interestingly, unlike most of its competitors, BA has adopted a strategy not of increasing the number of seats available, but of increasing the frequency of flights and the proportion of its business that is devoted to business class passengers. In other words, BA is not seeking to grow the number of passengers it carries but to change the mix of passengers to those paying higher fares. BA is changing its fleet to meet the new requirements (for example by phasing out larger Boeing 747's and replacing them with smaller and more economical 777s). This will also remove assets from the balance sheet so helping to boost reported profits. Other airlines, such as Lufthansa for example, are still seeking to grow the number of passengers that they carry. In addition, Lufthansa, like Swissair, is also developing a significant presence in the supply side (that is, the service end) of the business. The article notes that Swissair is likely to make more money from its interests in servicing airlines that it does from actually flying. The airlines that are dedicated to growing passenger numbers are the newly emerging low-cost airlines (for example RyanAir and Easyjet) who, because of their low fares, need to fill aircraft in order to make any profits. BA is now competing head-to-head with these low-cost carriers with the establishment of its own subsidiary Go.

The second element that impacts on the development of the international airline industry is government regulation. We're not thinking here of regulations designed to set safety standards in the industry, but of those rules and regulations which restrict foreign ownership of airlines and government control over routes and flights. Such regulations have a number of effects. First they preclude the entry of new players into the game. Second they may restrict new players, or existing players, from particular routes. In addition, as the article notes, they prevent international mergers between airlines. An open skies policy, which frees airlines to fly without government interference, would undoubtedly be in the interests of passengers in the short term. However, whether universal open skies and a relaxation of foreign ownership which it is thought will lead to higher degrees of concentration in the industry are in the long-run interests of airline customers is open to question. At present the airline industry is a good example of how an overarching regulatory framework which we discussed in Chapter 4, influences the development of an industry.

Competition between international airlines, that is the intensity of rivalry, is a key determinant of profitability in the industry. Suppliers to the industry appear to have little influence and buyers are in general disparate and diffuse to wield much power. However, one issue that the article has overlooked that may develop into a growing and emerging threat are advances in information and communications technology. It is possible to envisage that some business travel may reduce in the future as the quality and reliability of technologies such as video conferencing and live Internet events improves.

6.3 Telecommunications

Our next example comes from a subset of the telecommunications industry. After years of research and development Iridium's formation was announced in 1990 and the company floated in the US in 1997. The company started its mobile satellite telephone service (MSS) in November 1998. The MSS market is a subset of the mobile telephone market that has shown enormous growth in the last few years and is predicted to grow substantially over the next two years. The article estimates that the MSS market is approximately 2.5 per cent of the overall mobile telephone industry.

Illustration 6.3

Star Struck

Is Iridium about to fall to earth?

Its designers named Iridium after the 77th element in honour of the 77 satellites that were to beam signals around the world. In the event, the mobile-telephone network uses only 66 satellites, but Dysprosium, the 66th element, sounds more like an anti-depressant than a technological marvel.

Which is fitting. On July 14th Iridium's shares tumbled 18 per cent, to $6.75, on news that Motorola, which has already ploughed $1.66bn into the venture, has vowed not to invest any more unless other investors do so too. Over the past year Iridium's shares have fallen by

---

89 per cent. Little more than nine months since it opened for business, the world's first mobile satellite-telephone service (MSS) may already be doomed. Worse, Iridium's failing could tarnish the prospects of two better-conceived rival services. Globalstar, which will be launched later this year, and ICO, which will enter the market in August 2000.

Iridium's survival could depend upon whether Motorola's threats can get its investors, bond-holders and creditors to agree on the outlines of a financial restructuring before a deadline of August 11th. Separately, Iridium was due to make a $90m bond payment on July 15th, though it has a 30-day grace period. If it misses the payment or the haggling over restructuring drags on, the company could file for bankrupcy.

Equally critical will be whether the 65 per cent cut in the price of calls, announced at the end of June, has increased the number of subscribers from 10,000 at the end of March to the revised (though still modest) target of 27,000 by the end of July. Iridium is in a bind: investors won't put more money in until they see that customers are interested, whereas customers won't buy until they know the company has the financial backing to survive.

Rocket science

Iridium got itself into this mess astonishingly quickly. Were its estimates of the MSS market – between 32m and 45m subscribers within ten years – plain wrong? Or are Iridium's own failing chiefly responsible?

Iridium's assessment of the market still seems right. Mobile telephony is going from strength to strength. In the next two years, the number of subscribers world-wide is expected almost to double to nearly 600m. Analysts, such as Tom Watts of Merrill Lynch, a brokerage, think the MSS providers should be able to grab about 2.5 per cent of that by offering handsets that will operate as both a land-based cellular phone and a satellite telephone when cellular service is unavailable. ICO's most recent market research, spanning 12 countries and 20 000 interviews, confirms earlier findings that if the price is right, the demand will be there.

Apart from continent-hopping business executives, niche markets include long-haul truckers, civil engineers, field scientists, disaster-relief agencies, news organisations, extractive industries and geologists. Satellite telephones should also be useful in shipping and aviation, as well as in less-developed countries that lack either modern fixed-wire or wireless telephone infrastructures.

Yet Iridium has signed up pitifully few subscribers. Technology gremlins are not to blame, despite the launch being delayed a month or two by some software problems. Although they are complicated and expensive, Iridium's low-earth orbiting satellites have worked pretty much as billed. The real problem has been more prosaic: unimaginably bad marketing.

Well before Iridium was launched, there were concerns that the company was in danger of setting its prices too high. Iridium's handsets cost more than $3000 and call charges ranged for $2 to $7 a minute. Edward Staiano, Iridium's chief executive until he abruptly quit in April, believed that by being the first MSS firm, Iridium could charge a premium that would help pay for its over-budget $5bn platform.

To make matters worse, the Iridium handset is an off-putting brick seven in (18 cm) long, weighing 1 lb (450 g). It poignantly recalls the pioneering days of mobile phones a decade and a half ago. Even then Iridium's telephones were not available in the modest numbers needed. Manufacturing delays at Motorola and Kyocera left customers waiting until February to get their telephones. If they had been supplied earlier, the firm's distribution partners would probably not have been ready to sell them. Sprint, an American long-distance carrier, will begin its first promotional campaign soon – a good ten months after Iridium's launch; Telecom Italia, another lethargic distributor, is only now training its sales force to sell the devices.

An advertising campaign last year, costing $180m, was meant to bring in 500 000 customers by the end of March. Iridium's new chief executive, a blunt Australian called John Richardson, now describes its theme – 'Calling Planet Earth' – as 'schmoozy and generic' lifestyle marketing. Instead Iridium should have aimed its message at those who really need the service and given them lots of useful information. In the short-term, Iridium might salvage something. Its satellites are flying, the service works reasonably, the new tariffs are more realistic, the marketing will improve, and cheaper, better handsets are on their way.

There is, however, still a problem. ICO, Iridium's rival, calculates that, of the three MSS services, Iridium has by far the highest costs.

Assuming that each system carries 1bn minutes of calls a year, the cost of a minute using Iridium's system is $1.28 compared with 51 cents a minute for Globalstar and 35 cents for ICO.

The difference arises mainly because Iridium's satellites are both more numerous and use more power to maintain their low-earth orbits. They will thus need replacing within five to seven years of being launched. By comparison, ICO's ten satellites fly about 9,000 kilometres higher in medium-earth orbit and have a life-span of 12 years. With its prices already far lower than it had planned for and two lower-cost operators yet to enter the market, Iridium's future is questionable, even if it can battle through its current financial crisis.

Not that Globalstar and ICO are crowing over Iridium's difficulties. ICO, which went public last year, has seen its share price driven down from $16 $^1/_2$ to $5 as the scale of the Iridium debacle has become apparent. A rights issue intended to raise $500m failed to reach its target and has been extended to the end of July. ICO will probably succeed in raising the money, but only at greater cost.

And although even Iridium's Mr Richardson admits that 'we cocked it up', doubts about the size and value of the market for MSS will inevitably linger until more subscribers begin to appear. Nobody believes that $17bn-worth of the latest satellites will circle the globe ignored and in silence, but scarred investors can be excused if, in future, they take little on trust.

Source: The Economist, 17 July 1999

Iridium is the first company into the MSS market. The article estimates that the set up costs were approximately $5bn. Iridium has significant backing from Motorola and a number of other large strategic investors including American telecoms company Sprint, Telecom Italia and space systems and defence group Lockheed Martin. Motorola holds 18 per cent of the equity. Clearly the major investment required to get into this market is a significant barrier to entry. The service itself is targeted at a very particular customer for whom conventional mobile phones provide insufficient coverage. While there is no evidence that the estimates of potential are incorrect, that does not necessarily mean, as this case demonstrates, that there is a market in which it is possible to make sufficient returns to justify the significant capital investment required. In spite of the fact that this is a new service it seems clear that Iridium has not been able, for a variety of reasons, to attract sufficient subscribers due to poor marketing, inadequate distribution of the handsets, and perceived high prices for the service. Though the service may be unique, this would tend to indicate that potential users are comparing it with the ever cheaper cellular phone networks with which they are more familiar.

In this case technological change, especially in cellular phones, has always meant that the window of opportunity for MSS services was always narrow and getting narrower all the time. Advances in conventional cellular technology, for example the advent of UMTS, the next generation of mobile phones which will offer a single global standard, have also neutralized another selling point. Iridium provides a good example of an innovation which itself has been overtaken by developments in a related industry. Due to the slow uptake of its own MSS service, Iridium will it find difficult to resist these developments in the future.

This case also highlights the role that the company's share price plays in its ability to raise finance. In such a speculative venture the share price presumably reflects investors' collective view of likely future profitability. And while it may have been difficult to justify the higher historic values placed on Iridium shares, from the company's perspective this provided an umbrella within which it had the ability to raise future finance. The collapse of the share price makes raising finance more difficult and more costly. Iridium's shares reached a high of $70 in 1998. They were suspended in August 1999 at just over $3, when the company filed for protection under US bankruptcy laws. Iridium filed for Chapter 11 after its failure to agree terms with investors and bondholders who were owed $3bn, including Barclays Bank and the Royal Bank of Scotland. It had already defaulted on loans of $1.55 bn and bankruptcy beckons if they fail to agree a restructuring of its debts. While this is bad enough for the company itself, it has knock-on effects for its other two competitors in the industry ICO and Globalstar.

6.4 The Car Industry

Compared to mobile telephones or the manufacture of computers the car industry is a much older and more traditional industry. The mass production of automobiles has been carried out since the 1920s when Henry Ford set up the production line for the Model T. Since then the industry has undergone significant change and development: there have been a number of new entrants into the industry, particularly from Asia, as well as the demise of some manufacturers, or at least their brands. Illustration 6.4 sets out some of the issues by focusing on two manufacturers, Ford and Fiat.

Illustration 6.4

The Revolution at Ford

Jac Nasser wants to turn Ford Motor from the very symbol of mass production into a consumer-products and services company.

From Jac Nasser's window you can see the motor town that Henry Ford built. The skyline is dominated by the chimneys of his Old River Rouge steel mill and the iron guts of Detroit. But the offices of Ford's chief executive could not be less industrial: eight television screens line the back wall, above a bench with an open lap-top. On a window-sill sit two monitors displaying the websites of Ford and its competitors. CNBC business news burbles in the background; share prices and charts flicker; a coffee-machine wheezes in the corner. The most talked-about chief executive in America, *espresso* in hand, is at work in a weird, post-modern palace.

Ford is definitely fizzing. Mr Nasser has not dawdled since he took over in January (with Bill Ford as non-executive chairman, custodian of the family's 40 per cent interest). Outsiders such as Wolfgang Reitzle, formerly number two at BMW, has been drafted in along with some of the brightest Chrysler talent, unhappy to play second fiddle to the dominant Daimler executives.

Ford's financial results look impressive too, thanks largely to its consumer-finance arm and its best-selling range of light trucks. The Ford F-series truck, in its various guises, brings in sales of $60bn, more than a third of the company's total. But Ford nevertheless has problems. Apart from finance and trucks, says David Cole, of the University of Michigan, 'nothing else is working'. Mr Ford himself admits that passenger cars in America 'need fixing'.

Mr Nasser is clear about what he must do: he wants not only to strengthen the weak parts of the business, but also to turn Ford from a boring old car maker whose shares achieve a price-earnings ratio of only ten, into a consumer-products and services company commanding a multiple of more like 30. Ford's marketing supremo, Jim Schroer, formerly the number two at RJR Nabisco, a leading consumer-products company, describes the rewards thus: 'Auto companies are seen as firms which invest a lot and get little return. Consumer companies are seen as investing little and earning a lot'.

The first thing Mr Nasser plans is to diversify into services related to cars. This is the idea behind Ford's recent purchase of the Kwik-Fit exhausts and brakes chain in Europe, its acquisition of scrapyard businesses in America and the deal this week to buy the consumer-finance arm of Japan's Mazda. It has even signed a deal to provide drivers with satellite-fed audio and other services for a monthly fee. These sit alongside the firm's huge existing consumer-finance business and its Hertz car-rental subsidiary. Whereas car makers are lucky to scrape operating margins of more than 5 per cent from actually making cars, other businesses such as leasing, renting, insurance, finance and car repair, can all achieve margins of 10–15 per cent.

With this shift of emphasis, Ford will pursue profits right down the value-chain of the car industry. It will also try to sell its low-margin in-house parts company, Visteon (a move that is unpopular with Ford workers and may lead to a strike in North America). Following the lead taken by General Motors at its 'Blue Macaw' factory in Rio Grande do Sul in Brazil, Ford is also trying to get suppliers to sub-assemble more of its cars, and may eventually even subcontract final assembly.

But the more demanding task facing Mr Nasser, if he is to turn Ford into a consumer company, is to fix Ford's brand management. Despite the money that the industry spends on advertising, few car firms have a strong grasp of their brands. The outstanding exception is BMW, whose customers identify with its slogan, 'the ultimate driving machine', and like to think it applies to them as drivers. (That is why Mr Nasser hired Mr Reitzle shortly after he left BMW in February following a boardroom row.)

Ford's previous upheaval, called Ford 2000, addressed the nuts-and-bolts of manufacturing and was designed to merge the company's regional fiefs into a $150bn global company. In contrast, Mr Nasser's latest drive at Ford is supposed to exploit brands to sweat every dollar that the firm spends on product development, research and engineering. By spreading the fixed cost of investment across a variety of attractive cars, all made from the same kits of parts, the investment should deliver higher returns.

But that will work only if Ford can package combinations of similar components as distinct brands, such as Ford, Lincoln, Jaguar or Volvo, each with its consumer appeal. Mr Nasser hopes that importing the technique of consumer-marketing to product development will make all models look, drive and feel the essence of the different brands that Ford has promoted – even when their underlying engineering is the same.

Ford certainly needs to do something. If you want to provoke the diminutive, dynamic Mr Nasser, you have only to compliment him about Ford's financial results and then commiserate with him about its performance in the American car market; its disastrous experiences in South America, after the break-up of its Brazilian joint venture with Volkswagen; and its lacklustre record in Europe, where it is plagued by overcapacity.

Mr Nasser retorts by pointing to pickups and sport – utility vehicles in America (known as light trucks), now the firm's biggest money-spinner. After Ford put four doors on its basic F-150 pick up truck ('when in doubt, add a door' is a Ford maxim – because Mr Nasser decreed it), its huge sales of 750 000 a year were swollen with fancier versions, some bearing the Lincoln brand. These gas-guzzlers seem almost as big as a small European house – greens call the latest of them, the nearly six metre-long Excursion, the 'Ford Valdez'. They earn Ford profits of more than $10 000 apiece, because, although they look and feel extravagant, the basic engineering is that of the old pick-up. This is just the sort of trick that Ford wants to repeat across its mainstream passenger cars.

Detours and mistakes

It needs to. Although Ford 2000 put Ford's product development on a global basis, the idea has not worked so far. Its American versions of the Mondeo (conceived in Europe) were a flop. Ford managed to sell the Ford Contour and Mercury Mystique (dubbed by Detroit wags as the 'Detour' and the 'Mistake'), but only by discounting heavily. The cars, as Mr Nasser admits, were not 'correctly positioned', because they were too expensive for their segment.

But such failures relate to the old Detroit ways of selling cars, which was to arm-twist dealers and consumers with special offers to "move the metal', backed by big, crude advertising campaigns. The first test of the new Ford approach to marketing will be the Ford Focus, which it showed off to America's motoring press last week in New Hampshire. This is the replacement for the Escort; it is the first product to be developed entirely since Ford 2000. Its hard-edged, stylish looks have gone down well in Europe, but they risk being too outlandish for elderly Americans who need to save money, or affluent families looking for a second or third car.

Hence Ford hopes it can use its new consumer-marketing techniques to appeal to young Americans. The brains behind this approach is Mr Schroer, who thinks that complex and expensive things like cars make far better consumer products than toothpaste and ketchup. Out goes the big launch and advertising blitz. Instead Ford is planning a phased roll-out of the car, with publicity on the Internet and sponsorship of adventure sports and live music. The idea is that young customers whose parents will be buying them their first car will think that the Focus (and hence Ford) is 'cool'.

The gossip around Detroit is that Mr Nasser is driving his executive team too hard. Few can match his phenomenal energy. He gets by on three hours of sleep a night, and has been known to fly to Europe so he can keep working over American holidays. Returning on Saturday afternoon from a trip to Europe or Asia with a small group of managers, he is likely to suggest they all drop by the design studio before heading home.

Yet the more Mr Nasser exhausts his executives, the more he impresses industry analysts, many of whom now say that Ford has a chance of becoming the biggest car maker in the world, a position it lost in the 1920s to General Motors. Bill Ford denies that this is the target, saying that size is the result of success rather than an aim in itself. The company will be 100 years old in 2003. World leadership would be a fitting way to celebrate.

Friendless Fiat?

'Everybody is talking to everybody else. We are too busy assimilating Volvo, but you should never say never. That is how Bill Ford, chairman of Ford Motor, sums up Ford's view of the current consolidation in the car industry. The pairing off of Renault and Nissan in March re-launched the speculation that first began with the merger between Daimler and Chrysler last year.

The name that refuses to go away is Fiat. Rumours of its desperate search for a partner are buzzing in Detroit and came to a head in Turin in mid-July, when the company held a 100th-birthday bash attended by such celebrities as Henry Kissinger, along with car industry luminaries such as Daimler Chrysler's Jürgen Schrempp. Cue rumours of Fiat courting Daimler Chrysler. Or perhaps Ford. Had the Agnelli family, which owns about a third of the company, wanted to make a quick killing, it should have taken advantage of the birthday spike in the share price, as the sycophantic Italian media wove merger speculation into their hagiographies.

Behind all this is a grim necessity: the Agnellis have to do something about Fiat Auto. In areas such as robotics, farm and construction machinery and lorries, Fiat is now world-class. Indeed, according to the rumours in Milan, it had hoped to seal a purchase of American Navistar, a lorry firm, to add lustre to the birthday party.

By contrast, Fiat Auto is too small; it makes fewer than 2.5m cars a year, just over half as many as Volkswagen, the leading European car maker and the only one with global reach. The Italian company is strong only in Europe and South America. But margins are squeezed by overcapacity in Europe, and the state of the Brazilian economy has ruined the car market there. Despite bold statements about being predator not prey, Fiat needs a friend, and it is not having much luck finding one.

Fiat is now chaired by Paolo Fresco, formerly deputy to Jack Welch at General Electric and a man well-versed in corporate wheeling and dealing. Since he arrived, the company's share price has gyrated to the rhythm of the rumour mill about possible partners. The Turin-based company has been trying for a year to buy BMW, only to be rebuffed; its latest gambit was to offer the Munich managers its Alfa Romeo, Lancia and Ferrari brands to run as a premium-car division, the way that Ford handles Jaguar and Volvo.

Fiat had already failed in its bid to buy the whole of Volvo (lorries and all) earlier this year. But the Italians, realising that the only of kind of partner that makes sense must have a North American presence, also knocked on the door of General Motors. The deal was that Fiat Auto would be hived off and GM would take a one-third stake: the Italians argued that both companies shared big problems in South America and Europe, and combining forces would make sense. GM listened respectfully, but apparently declined to go any further.

Source: The Economist, 7 August 1999

There appears to be significant over-capacity in the industry. In recent years there have been a number of takeovers and mergers; for example Daimler/Chrysler, Ford acquiring Volvo and the partnership between Renault and Nissan. This indicates that rivalry between car makers is intense. There were some new entrants into European car making in the 1980s, primarily from Japan, whose entry was eased by generous government subsidies to establish factories, and hence reduce unemployment, in depressed areas of the UK (for example, Sunderland, Derby and Swindon). In addition, the article above stresses the need to spread central (and fixed) costs, such as research and development, engineering, and so on across the whole range of vehicles that a firm makes. So scale economies are clearly important in this industry. The Ford case is interesting because it throws some light on the company's profitability. The F series Truck, in selling 750 000 units per annum, provides a third of total revenues ($60bn) and a significant chunk of profit. Consumer finance appears to provide most of the rest. So there are serious issues in terms of the profitability of the manufacture of its other ranges of cars and the nature of its marketing. In order to tackle some of these problems, Ford like GM is thinking of getting its suppliers to sub-assemble automobiles. The question is even raised as to whether or not whole cars might be assembled by suppliers or subcontractors. This naturally then leads into discussing the type of company that a car maker is. Ford's diversification into car-related services, such as the acquisition of Kwik-Fit in Europe, is good evidence of the company's move into higher margin businesses. If moves such as this are replicated by other competitors it would mark another step-change in the development of the industry.

Given the over-capacity in the industry, coupled with intense rivalry, and given the difficulty therefore for new entrants (unless supported by government subsidies), the industry itself might face competition in the area of substitutes for personal transport. Here the industry is under a lot of pressure from environmental lobbyists who wish to see the use of cars reduced. For example, the road construction programme in the UK has virtually ceased as a consequence of these pressures. Public transport is another alternative that would require significant further investment to act as a realistic challenger to the convenience of using a car. However, the industry does itself no favours with the arrangements it has with its dealers across Europe. Again in the UK, the Competition Commission found that Volvo have been fixing prices in its dealerships; the OFT has ordered an investigation into why UK prices for the same car are considerably higher than European prices. There is no obvious reason why the price of a Ford Focus should be one third lower in Belgium than in the UK.

The ownership of major car manufacturers is also of interest. The Ford family still owns a considerable percentage of Ford, the Agnelli family owns a substantial part of Fiat, and the Quandt family still has an effective controlling interest in BMW. We raise these points because such entrenched family interests are likely to look at the future of the company in a slightly different way to that of more financially orientated stockmarket investors. That is, they may be willing for psychological reasons to take a longer-run view of the ultimate return to themselves as shareholders than institutional investors who have comparative performance indicators for their investment funds to worry about.

6.5 Retailing

In Chapter 3 we considered the evidence on concentration, particularly among food and clothing retailers in Europe. We noted that there was considerable evidence that such retailers exerted considerable influence over their supply chains. We also noted that in many cases competition between retailers was perhaps not as intense as one might expect, due to the effect of planning constraints for superstores. Illustration 6.5 below sets out some of the issues for retailers' international activities. In reading through this particular example it is important to recall that retailers are now some of the largest organizations in terms of turnover, capital employed, and number of employees, in the world.

Illustration 6.5

Shopping All Over the World

Retailers are trying to go global. They will struggle to succeed.

At first glance, Wal-Mart's £6.7bn ($10.7bn) bid for Asda, announced on June 14th, is a huge threat both to British supermarkets and to the rest of Europe's retailing elite. But the American firm's triumph was marred by a tiff close to home. On the day it swooped on Asda, Bob Martin, Wal-Mart's long-standing international head, resigned unexpectedly. Although Mr Martin was passed over for the top job at Wal-Mart in January, the timing of his departure suggests that, just as the world's most powerful retailer is seeking to double its international sales, it is divided about how far and how fast to push globalisation.

Global Cross-Border Retail Mergers and Acquisitions

	No. of deals	Approx. value $bn
1990	100	6.0
1991	136	2.8
1992	135	3.0
1993	152	10.0
1994	186	4.5
1995	230	6.0
1996	208	12.5
1997	214	13.0
1998	268	16.0
1999 (year to 16 June)	126	18.0

Wal-Mart's British acquisition comes at a time when retailers have caught globalisation fever. They are behind most manufacturers, but the bug is the more virulent for that. In the past several months, Royal Ahold, a Dutch supermarket operator, has bought supermarkets in Poland, four rival chains in Spain, one in America and two in Argentina. France's leading hypermarket, Carrefour, which is in 20 markets, has opened stores in Chile, Colombia, Indonesia and the Czech Republic; it recently announced that it would move into Japan next year. Tesco,

Britain's biggest food retailer, has set up shop in South Korea, its sixth overseas market. And Promodès, another French hypermarket group, has become the market leader in Argentina. Meanwhile, fast-growing clothes chains, such as The Gap, Sweden's Hennes & Mauritz (in 12 markets), and Spain's Zara (in 17), are opening a branch in a new country every few weeks. Despite this enthusiasm, however, retailers seem to be finding it hard to make a success of the transition from national to multinational. Although a few firms, such as IKEA, a Swedish furniture retailer, have done well, established international retailers still make most of their money and their highest returns at home (see chart below). Carrefour's operating margins in France are more than 6 per cent of sales, whereas, after operating internationally for 30 years, it still loses money in much of Asia, Latin America and even some parts of Europe. Meanwhile Wal-Mart, which first went abroad in 1991, makes a return on capital of 5.8 per cent on its international business, far lower than in America. Can today's headlong rush succeed?

Home is where the cart is

Selected global retailer	Home country	Sales 1998, $bn	% of sales overseas	No of countries	Market capitalisation June 15th, $bn
Wal-Mart	USA	150.7	17	10	199.7
Royal Ahold	Netherlands	37.1	71	17	22.0
Promodes	France	36.2	54	12	12.6
Carrefour	France	36.0	44	20	30.5
Home Depot	USA	30.2	neg.	4	84.5
Tesco	UK	28.4	13	9	19.5
Marks & Spencer	UK	13.3	16	34	16.8
Toys 'Я' Us	USA	11.2	27	26	5.3
Pinault Printemps	France	10.0	30	23	19.3
Hennes & Mauritz	Sweden	3.4	82	12	17.9

One reason for scepticism is that retailers are being driven by slow growth at home as much as by the sight of opportunities abroad, according to Felix Barber of Boston Consulting Group (BCG) in Zurich. The small size of the Swedish market encouraged several of the country's retailers to move overseas as early as the 1970s. A few, such as IKEA and Hennes, have built strong international businesses, although they have taken years to do so. French retailers, such as Carrefour and Auchan, have gone into emerging markets to escape the constraints of planning laws. Even Wal-Mart, which is still producing sales growth in America, is going abroad partly because it already has a dominant share of the country's non-food market.

Shop flaws

As everybody piles in abroad, the opportunities are dwindling. Many local retailers in Latin America have either been bought or are already in joint ventures. The price of those that remain is rising. Multinationals are snapping up partners all over Asia – witness Carrefour's recent move into Japan.

However, retailers assert that globalisation is about more than simply adding to their turnover. Sir Geoff Mucahy, boss of Kingfisher, which launched an earlier, lower bid for Asda, argues that the main reason retailers want new sales is to exploit economies of scale and to spread the rising costs of marketing and technology. In Europe, international scope may also help retailers to cope with the single currency, which will make it easier for consumers to compare prices across borders.

In practice, however, international scale economies are hard to achieve. In the excitement of their charge into new markets, many retailers forget that the crucial ingredient of their success at home is their relative size and market share. Without enough sales and profits in a particular market, even the most long-term management will find it difficult to justify the expense of setting up a large distribution network or installing the latest technology – and without these, the international newcomer cannot compete with entrenched locals. In America, Carrefour opened a mere three stores in Pennsylvania, and abandoned its investment before getting anywhere near the scale needed.

The secret may be to arrive in force. Ahold, which has bought itself a concentrated market share on America's East Coast, is doing well. So is Carrefour in Spain, where the French firm is now the second-largest retailer. Ahold's frantic recent purchases in Spain are an attempt to catch up, though it still has less than 1 per cent of the market.

Cross-border scale economies are particularly elusive in food retailing – precisely where overseas expansion has been most enthusiastic, notes Keith Wills, a retail analyst at Goldman Sachs in London. BCG's Mr Barber says that almost all retailers overestimate the scope for savings from aggregating lots of local orders for a product into a single world-wide contract. Few deals manage to produce even 1–2 per cent of sales in savings.

The reason is partly that the biggest suppliers have not yet woken up to such 'global sourcing'. Meredith Prichard, J.P. Morgan's Latin American retailing analyst, argues that Procter & Gamble's priority in say, Brazil, is not going to be Wal-Mart, but CBD, the country's biggest retailer. 'P&G's managers negotiate locally, their goods are made locally and their internal targets are local,' she adds.

In time, world-wide contracts will become more widespread – P&G this month announced plans to reorganize itself along global lines. However, the regional managers of suppliers are unlikely to embrace global sourcing with enthusiasm. Ira Kalish, a retail analyst at PricewaterhouseCoopers, predicts that as suppliers succumb to pressure from retailers, perhaps a third of a supermarket's lines could be sourced globally or regionally in five years, up from less than 10 per cent now.

Yet global sourcing is no panacea, because it conflicts with the need to cater to local tastes. Stores in different countries stock very different goods, which undermines the point of global sourcing and complicates relations between local and global managers – of both the retailer and its supplier.

Local taste crucially affects the way retailers sell their goods too. In 1996 Wal-Mart set up efficient, clean supercentres in Indonesia, only to find that Indonesians preferred Matahari, the shabbier shop next door, which reminded shoppers of a street market where they can haggle and buy the freshest fruit and vegetables. Two years later, Wal-Mart pulled out. Boots, a British pharmacy, found the number of visitors to its Thai shops soared after it started playing pop-music videos at full volume. Customers had found the shops too quiet. And when Boots opens in Japan this July, staff at the checkout will be standing up —its research has shown that Japanese shoppers find it offensive to pay money to seated staff.

Trouble in store

Even concepts that have global appeal need local tinkering. Jose Castellano, the chief executive of Zara, insists that 'as tastes for music and television have gone global, so has fashion'. Yet MTV, the epitome of a global media brand, decided to adapt its musical mix to local markets. Equally, Zara has lost sales in Britain, because its sizing is considered too small for the British figure.

If they are to overcome such obstacles, multinational retailers need a fanatical attention to detail, and a willingness to do whatever local whim dictates. Wal-Mart had to abandon its attempt to sell Brazilians (cheaper) Colombian coffee: they insist on drinking their own. IKEA tried to sell Americans its own beds, before discovering that they were the wrong size for their bedlinen; sales of its four-legged desks to Germans also flopped – five legs are preferred.

One way of getting an inside track on local tastes is to join a local partner, something that in many developing countries is required by law. But even that often leads to conflict, since many big Western retailers think they know better. In Brazil, Wal-Mart failed to tap the local knowledge of its joint-venture partner, Logas Americanas. Failing to spot that most families have one car and shop at the weekends, Wal-Mart built car parks and store aisles that were too small to accommodate the weekend rush. Because many joint ventures fail, local firms are reluctant to give up trade secrets or surrender their best sites. After all, they could be competitors again within a few years.

Yet multinational retailers do have some advantages. Know-how is probably the greatest, according to Cees van der Hoeven, the chief executive of Ahold. At its heart, this is a sophisticated understanding of supply chains, beginning with electronic links to suppliers who can tell instantaneously what customers are buying at the checkout. The next, much trickier, stage is to persuade suppliers to share information with both retailers and rivals, so that they can minimize inventory and put more of what customers want on the shelves.

If cultures are similar or the retailer is established, it is relatively easy for suppliers to accept new buying systems and new technology, and this can lead to savings. Following a flurry of acquisitions in America, Ahold USA expects to save around $85m this year and $115m in 2000. Similarly, Wal-Mart should be able to improve Asda's supply-chain management and make better use of its floorspace. Meanwhile, 7-Eleven, a chain of convenience stores that is Japan's most successful retailer, is starting to apply its expertise to stores in Hawaii.

However, even best practice is hindered by cultural differences. Wal-Mart has worked with Grupo Cifra, a Mexican retailer, since 1991 and has had a controlling stake for the past two years, but only recently introduced a modern till-information system (years after local rivals had installed one). So far, it has had little effect on margins, as employees are still learning how to use it. Because labour is so cheap, local managers are loath to announce the layoffs that the new technology allows. Similarly, new owners often meet resistance when they try to get their new subsidiary to cut links that were established with suppliers over many years.

Given that globalisation is fraught with such difficulties, which sort of retailers will make a good fist of it?

The leaders so far are 'category killers' with a strong focus, products with universal appeal and their own brands. The Gap, with its khakis and white shirts, and the IKEA furniture chain combine large volumes with higher margins and control over their design, distribution and sourcing. Some Internet retailers may turn out to fall into this group too, though maintaining a global brand over the long-haul could prove cripplingly expensive for what are, after all, loss-making start-ups. And the international failures of Britain's Laura Ashley and Body Shop, and America's Toys 'R' Us show what happens if expansion abroad is not carefully managed.

Food and general-merchandise retailers have a harder job. Crucially, they must dominate their home base, as do both Wal-Mart and Ahold – but as Promodès does not. Otherwise they will find it difficult to pay for their expansion. They also need to offer a variety of formats, from convenience stores to supermarkets and hypermarkets, in order to ensure market coverage.

On the shop front

Most important, a general retailer needs a strong brand if consumers are to trust it with their personal details or buy its higher-margin products and services. Tesco and 7-Eleven Japan have successfully used information from loyalty cards to adapt their stores, products and prices to local tastes and to move into services such as banking and bill payments. A recent survey by CLK, a market-research group, shows that trusted retail brands have great power: a third of the 1000 British adults surveyed said they would buy a house from an estate agent with a supermarket brand; 15 per cent would buy a supermarket-branded car. Boots is trusted by 85 per cent of young people in Britain (only 10 per cent have the same feeling for the royal family).

Yet, a well-known brand takes a great deal of time to create – partly because, unlike manufacturers, whose products are promoted by shops, retailers must do all the promoting themselves. As Marc Berman, an analyst at Euromonitor in London notes: 'Most retailers entering new markets are unknowns to suppliers and customers. Building trust takes years.'

Despite the time and the investment that will be needed, a small group of rich firms with skilled managers will probably succeed. They may even be able to pay over the odds for 'strategic' acquisitions – as Wal-Mart is doing with Asda – if this allows them eventually to dominate markets. British and continental European retailers are, in this sense, right to fear the arrival of Wal-Mart on their shores. Bur for many other retailers, the hoped-for economies of scale from globalisation will prove elusive. Local tastes will often get in the way; best practice will take frustratingly long to put into action. No doubt managers will persist in trying to go global. But too often they will be motivated less by the chance of creating value than by the fear of being left out and gobbled up themselves.

Source: The Economist, 19 June 1999

The article above claims that the main driver for retailers' international expansion has been slow growth in their own home market. The article also notes that successful retailers' relative size and market share in their home arena is one of the key determinants of success. This makes international expansion more problematic since starting with a small base in another country will not be a worthwhile strategy to pursue. The article reinforces the point made in Chapter 3 on the constraints caused by overarching planning regulations; in this case they were one of the drivers for French retailers developing internationally. Another driver for international expansion relates to scale economies. But here the evidence is mixed in terms of the ability to achieve scale economies in international retailing. The only retailers that seem to have been able to achieve this are those that are tightly focused, such as The Gap and IKEA. It is also difficult to imagine how scale economies can be achieved with perishable foodstuffs. Unlike other industries, for example the car industry that we discussed above, global sourcing of inputs does not appear to be very developed so far. It is estimated that global sourcing may provide up to a third of the international retailers' goods within the next five years. The main advantage that major retailers have in expanding internationally relate to know-how, particularly in relation to management of the supply chain.

A further point relates to brand recognition. The article notes that trusted retail brands have great power. Paradoxically, building a brand takes a great deal of time for a retailer because, unlike manufacturers whose products are promoted by shops, retailers must do all the promotion themselves. Another challenge that is likely to face retailers in the future comes from Internet shopping. This may be a particular challenge for clothing retailers as it is quite likely that orders for standard clothing items such as underwear, jeans or shirts, where people know their size and buy the same goods at regular intervals, are easier to move onto the net. Even for Internet shopping, however, the brand is likely to be the attraction.

The image of the large retailer is not without problems. In America Wal-Mart is coming under criticism from those sections of society who wish to rediscover the virtues of small-town America, including mom-and-pop stores. Opponents of the company paint Wal-Mart as a giant monopoly sapping life out of American towns. In fact, there are a number of cases where the advent of superstores has had a detrimental effect on the local community in the long term. There are instances of whole communities having to travel 20–30 miles to the nearest store after the local Wal-Mart closed down, having already killed off the local competition. The dilemmas raised by its success – masterly efficiency in the service of consumer needs versus the hidden social cost of satisfying them, should give pause for thought. Closer to home there is some evidence that shoppers are not so enamoured of their shopping experiences. The Guardian published a survey noting that 55 per cent of shoppers were unable to name one store or chain they regarded as excellent and would be prepared to recommend to friends or family (Guardian 3 April, 1999). De Kare Silver (1998) noted that 16 per cent of consumers said that they generally dislike shopping, and that consumer acceptance of non-store retailing was already high, – 45 per cent of US households and 58 per cent of UK households purchased from published catalogues or by television each year.

These developments happen at a time when retailers are subject to considerable criticism for their power over consumers. Price differences across the European Union are difficult to justify. The following example demonstrates that British CenterParcs can cost more than twice as much as their European counterparts.

Table 6.1 *Holiday Prices across the European Union*

Country	August 6	October 15	December 20
United Kingdom	846	576	702
France	576	387	659
Holland	623	513	363
Belgium	496	460	324

Prices show the £ sterling cost of a two bedroom chalet sleeping four people for one week at CenterParcs in Longleat (UK), les Hauts de Bruyeres (France), Het Heijderbos (Holland) and Erperheide (Belgium).

Source: Sunday Times 23 May 1999

The Sunday Times of 16 May 1999 published a chart comparing prices for IKEA furniture in the UK and France under the headline of 'British pay up to 75 per cent more at IKEA than the French'. The table indicated that most items were considerably cheaper in France than they were in the UK. Retailers have claimed that such comparisons are over-simplistic and point to different land values, transport costs and so on, that affect operating costs differently across Europe. However, research suggests that despite some national and regional variations in the cost of labour in retailing and the rental for retail premises neither is large enough to explain the observed price dispersion (Dobson and Waterson, 1999).

7 The Way Ahead

In this our final chapter we want to do three things. First we will revisit some of the key themes that we have analysed and discussed in the book so far. Second, we will look at the impact of developments in information and communication technologies for both consumers and producers. Finally, we conclude the book by speculating on changes that are likely to happen in the future.

7.1 Revisiting Consumers and Competition

We started the book by considering the changing nature of competition. You may recall that we looked at the shifting boundaries in the media industry where the distinctions between film producers, TV companies, hardware manufacturers and so on, are becoming blurred. We also considered in an intro-ductory way some of the elements of globalization. Having introduced some of the key elements we then sought to analyse the views of consumers. How do we behave in purchasing products and services? We discussed issues concerning price and value, perceptions of quality, and concluded by developing a unique and straightforward framework for understanding consumer choice better. Our attention then shifted to consider the nature of markets. We looked at driving forces for change and sought to clarify our understanding of how competition develops and evolves and works in the real world. The discussion of the relationship between consumers and suppliers is not complete without considering the role of the regulatory authorities, both national and supranational. Our focus here was primarily on legislation designed to ensure and protect competitive markets. We also considered the influence of developments in the world's environment in terms of the use of resources and so on. We then moved on to consider strategic aspects of firms' supply chains. This returned us to aspects of globalization discussed earlier as we observed that many large organizations not only sourced raw materials or components on a world-wide basis, but also manufacture on a world-wide basis. We also noted that the globalization of supply chain management was a phenomenon that affected service organizations as well as manufacturers.

Having established the key parts of our discussion we then looked at how competition and consumers had faired in a variety of industries from personal computers to telecoms, to travel, cars, and retailing. The range of these examples enabled us to demonstrate some aspects of how competition has evolved over time. They also helped to identify those major forces that changed the nature of competition and hence markets, as well as setting out how the shifting nature of competition impacts on us all as consumers or buyers of the products or services. These examples also served to illustrate some of the moves that suppliers of goods and services are making together with the opportunities and constraints imposed on markets, and hence firms, generated by the regulatory authorities at national and international levels.

7.2 The Impact of Developments in Information and Communication Technologies

The revolution in the economics of information, brought about by technological advances such as the Internet, is radically changing the nature of competition. More than a third of European companies are using the Internet for marketing, and are making profitable sales. Internet transactions stand at more than 1 per cent of total commerce and are forecast to rise to almost 10 per cent by 2001 and more than 16 per cent by 2003. De Kare-Silver provides compelling evidence of the spread of the Internet and peoples ability to access it. He noted that: the number of host computers on the Net grew from 100000 in 1990 to 10m in 1995, with projections of 100m by the year 2000. He noted also that the number of commercial web sites grew from 350 in 1994 to 220000 in 1996, and that estimates for the year 2000 were for more than 1 m (De Kare-Silver, 1998, pp 51–58). Table 7.1 below shows the enormous growth and penetration of on-line households in a short period of time. Table 7.2 shows the degree of PC and internet penetration.

In considering the data in Table 7.2, European numbers are reminiscent of the American profile just one to two years ago. Countries that lag the US in online shopping face a number of challenges: the lack of adequate or cost-effective telecommunications; lack of an advanced credit system; and possibly most importantly, limited numbers of shopping sites written in their native language. Men tended to be the early adopters of Internet shopping; women are now 50 per cent of online shoppers in the US. While the percentages in Europe are currently considerably lower, it is likely that, just as women dominate shopping in most brick-and-mortar channels, in two years time they will assume a greater role in the virtual world.

Table 7.1   *On-line households, 1999 and 2005*

Country	1999	2005
USA	44.7	72.1
Europe	25.3	71.6
Asia	12.2	44.7
Japan	7.3	17.3
Australia	2.2	5.1
Germany	7.6	18.7
UK	4.7	12.6
France (excl. Minitel)	2.2	9.9
Scandinavia	4.2	6.6

Source: Jupiter Communications, 2000

Table 7.2   *PC and Internet shopping penetration*

	US	Canada	Australia	UK	Italy	France
Households with PC	53	56	47	41	14	26
Households that are on-line	34	39	22	29	5	14
Households that have shopped on-line	17	9	5	10	1	2

Source: 'Global Online Retailing', Ernst & Young, 2000

On-line shoppers are about 40 years old worldwide, they're also well educated, and have higher than average household incomes. So, they make an attractive group for firms to focus on as potential customers (Table 7.3).

Table 7.3 *Demographics of on-line buyers*

	US	Canada	Australia	UK	Italy	France
Age (mean)	41	42	38	37	37	35
Households income (wt. ave) in US$ (000)	59	50	62	65	36	48
% college grads & post-college	41	48	58	56	55	64

Source: 'Global Online Retailing', Ernst & Young, 2000

Table 7.4 lists the ten most popular Internet shopping categories.

Table 7.4 *Top Ten Internet Shopping Categories*

1	PC hardware
2	Travel
3	Entertainment
4	Books and music
5	Gifts and flowers
6	Apparel and footwear
7	Food and beverages
8	Jewellery
9	Sporting goods
10	Consumer electronics

Sources: 'From Computers to Croissants', Business Week, February1997; 'Internet Commerce', Forrester Research, 1997/98; 'Global Online Retailing', Ernst & Young, 2000

Figure 7.1 maps the items from Table 7.4 on to the framework we introduced in Chapter 2. Interestingly from this we can see that most of the items are high in search qualities with a relatively low amount of consumer involvement. The exceptions all being items high in experience attributes – travel, entertainment and consumer electronics which we might assume to have comparatively high involvement, and food and beverages which are assumed to have low involvement by consumers. Significantly there are no credence services at all, presumably because providers have yet to find ways of imparting sufficient knowledge of their offerings to overcome the difficulties potential consumers have in evaluating their service. Classifying items in this way is not a once and for all exercise. For example it is highly probable that, when they were introduced some 20 years ago, PCs were credence goods with a high level of involvement by the buyer. This was because their properties were not well understood and they were expensive items. The specifications of the PC were also subject to rapid change – think of the rate of change in their microprocessor and their software for example. At that time they were also sold predominantly to businesses. However, they are now so ubiquitous and their relative price has fallen to such an extent that they are now an item high in search qualities with a reasonable amount of customer involvement (on the basis that they cost on average around two weeks average income).

Customer Involvement

	High in Search Qualities	**High in Experience Qualities**	**High in Credence Qualities**
HIGH	Jewellery Gifts and flowers PC hardware	Travel Consumer electronics Entertainment	
LOW	Apparel and footwear Books and music Sporting goods	Food and beverages	

Easy to Evaluate ⟵——————————⟶ *Difficult to Evaluate*

Figure 7.1 *Understanding customer choice*

De Kare-Silver (2000, pp. 71–87) has also considered which goods and services lend themselves to the virtual world. The list he produced is very similar to the items identified above except that he also identified some basic financial services, such as car insurance, as having high potential for sale over the Internet. In his analysis he noted that approximately 80 per cent of customers' average grocery shopping baskets were made up of replenished items, there is therefore a high degree of familiarity with most of the weekly shop. He argues therefore that a wide range of what is currently sold in supermarkets could equally well be sold on-line without visiting a store. Connected to this is the reputation of the product for reliability and trust. A strong brand can create a depth and breadth of franchise that cuts across ages, demographics and geography. A strong brand may build commitment and loyalty that persuades consumers to pay more money for it because of its perceived value and reliability. So companies that have invested in their brands over time are in an excellent position to take advantage of future changes in shopping habits. For consumers learning to navigate their way through the Internet the easiest purchases will be the products they recognize or the brand names that have a track record.

The rate of change in the technology arena may present difficulties in understanding some of the fundamental shifts that are taking place. For example, the last few years have seen explosive growth in the use of the Internet for business to consumer and business to business transactions. This has primarily been based on the use of personal computers and communications networks. However, digital TV and Internet access using mobile telephones are in their infancy but are sure to have an impact particularly for the business to consumer sector. Christensen and Tedlow (2000) argue that the Internet is in effect a fourth retailing disruption, which is following the patterns established earlier. They identified two clear patterns in the way the earlier retailing disruptions unfolded. First, generalist stores and catalogues dominated retailing at the outset of the disruptions, but specialist retailers eventually supplanted them. The specialist emerged once the market for the new form of retailing had grown large enough to generate enough sales volume from a narrower but deeper product mix. Second, the disruptive retailers weighted their initial merchandizing mix toward products they could sell themselves – that is goods high in search and experience qualities which were simple, branded products whose key attributes could be comprehended visually and numerically. They then shifted their merchandize mix toward higher margin more complex products to maintain their profits in the face of intense competition at the low end of their business. Christensen and Tedlow point out that leading Internet retailers, such as Amazon.com, have already migrated towards the department store strategy. They see clear parallels between this and the historic development of Sears and Marshall Field, and argue that, despite the uncertainty involved, the odds will tend to favour specialists rather than generalists. In terms of identifying upmarket momentum the authors note that the Internet can enable retailers to communicate rich information about a broad set of complex products to very large sets of potential customers, which should enable them to move up-market more quickly than their predecessors did. Their final point is perhaps of most importance. They note that historically experts have under-estimated the ultimate reach of disruptive technologies. This is because they are blinded by their perception of the initial limitations of the new technology and so failed to appreciate the strength of the innovators' motivation to move from the fringes of commerce to the mainstream.

Illustration 7.1 below indicates how one of the world's largest retailers is attempting to utilize the Internet. Interestingly, in the light of what we have discussed so far, the entry of Wal-Mart into this arena is fascinating because in the US Wal-Mart's regular shoppers tend to have lower incomes than the average and hence much lower than those who have thus far shopped on-line. In addition, the short article notes Microsoft's ambition to 'make the web as prevalent as the telephone', an ambition which is also shared by Sun Microsystems who talk of 'webtone' (that is, the equivalent of a telephone's dial tone).

Illustration 7.1

AOL/Wal-Mart

Wal-Mart, the world's largest retailer, and America Online, the largest interact services company, joined the race to open up the internet to a broader range of users yesterday, unveiling plans for a low-cost, co-branded internet service provider.

The much-trailed alliance was announced as Microsoft agreed a $200m investment in Best Buy, the consumer electronics retailer, and signed a joint marketing alliance under which Best Buy will promote its MSN Internet access product and Microsoft will advertise BestBuy.com to its 40m users.

Wal-Mart and AOL intend to charge a fee for Internet access, but would not say how much this would be. Some analysts said this decision could put the pair at a disadvantage to Kmart and Yahoo, which announced a free internet access service earlier this week.

Bob Pittman, president of AOL, cast doubt on the prospects of free Internet service providers, however, saying he doubted others would have the network to handle the traffic.

Paul Merenbloom, of Prudential Securities, added: 'The combination of Wal-Mart's pricing, AOL's ease of use and near ubiquitous reach suggest a pending *tsunami* (or tidal wave) of e-commerce, benefiting the consumer and each of the companies.'

To date, higher-income households have been disproportionately heavy users of the Internet. That fact posed a problem for Wal-Mart's e-commerce ambitions, analysts said, as many of the retailer's 92m regular shoppers have lower incomes and live in rural communities where Internet penetration is relatively low.

According to Media Metrix, a market research group, 17m online shoppers with incomes between $40,000 and $60,000 visited online shopping sites in October. By contrast, 8.6m shoppers in the $60,000–$75,000 income bracket and 18.3m in the $75,000–$150,000 bracket shopped online.

Microsoft, which has already signed a similar alliance with RadioShack, the electronics retailer, said the partnership with Best Buy would help it achieve its vision of 'making the web as prevalent as the telephone'.

The model of technology companies partnering with established consumer brands to promote their products and services among a broader audience could be applied to other technologies such as wireless telephones, analysts believe.

Wal-Mart would not comment on any such plans, but said that the co-branded version of AOL's Compuserve internet access service would be available from the first quarter of next year.

Source: Financial Times 17 December 1999

Ghosh (1998) identified four types of business opportunities presented by the Internet. First, firms can establish direct links to customers. Second, the technology lets companies bypass other competitors in the value chain. Third, companies can use the Internet to develop and deliver new products and services for new customers. Fourth, a firm could conceivably use the Internet to become the dominant player in the digital channel of a specific industry or segment. Dell Computers provides an example of the competitive impact of such technology-based distribution strategies. Michael Dell, its founder and CEO, has noted that the direct model favoured by Dell allowed them to leverage relationships with both suppliers and customers to such an extent that they have become virtually integrated. Furthermore, their approach substitutes information for inventory, which also reduces risk (Magretta, 1998).

Consider Illustration 7.2 below. This provides some insight into the impact of technology, primarily on marketing, but also on other aspects of e-commerce. For example, it is interesting to note how direct marketing can be traced back to the local shopkeeper who has largely disappeared today. Perhaps the key point is how the piece demonstrates that, by using the latest technologies, it is possible to understand consumers' purchasing patterns and their needs better. While this may be fine for suppliers it does raise interesting issues in terms of privacy and data protection. It also links to the issues raised in Chapter 5 concerning the development of flexible manufacturing systems designed to cater for changing customer needs and expectations.

Illustration 7.2

Direct Hit

Direct marketing, focused on individual customers, has become a potent way to sell. Should consumers worry?

Think of the junk mail clogging your letterbox, or those annoying cold calls during supper, and direct marketing seems a modern curse. That is because so much of it is so crude. But behind those resistible offers and fake prize-draws lies an important change in marketing. This is a move away from mass marketing, which starts with a product and finds customers to buy it, towards an information-led, one-to-one marketing, which may ultimately sell each individual a customised product.

The catalyst for this change is computer technology. Its falling costs and increasing power are allowing 'mass-customised' manufacturing, the gathering and manipulation of vast amounts of personal data and, for the first time, a ready way for customers to tell producers directly want they think, increasingly in real time. The consequence are huge. With near-perfect information, direct marketing has the potential to deliver near-perfect customer service.

But might it also lead to an age when no private detail is safe? At the end of October, the European Union implemented a data protection directive that gives consumers the legal right to check on information about them and to prevent its use. Moreover, the EU threatens to prevent countries with less strict data-protection guidelines – including the United States – from using data on European consumers. Within the next few months, the argument could descend into a trade war. What is at stake?

Direct descendants

The new form of direct marketing is a big step up from today's crude version. But it is also in some ways a step back. The first direct marketers were trusted local shopkeepers. Compared with today's direct marketers, whose best stab at intimacy is a pre-printed letter with a mis-spelt name, the local shopkeeper really knew his customers – remembering when to order a favourite bolt of fabric for one, suggesting a new cough tincture to another. 'He carried his database in his head,' says Don Peppers, who with Martha Rogers was an early advocate of personalised marketing.

The transformation of direct marketing from its local origins into advertising's downmarket cousin dates from the birth of mass production, which enabled manufacturers to produce goods in large quantities for sale by chain stores to unseen buyers. Lester Wunderman, inventor of the term 'direct marketing', believes that mass production has conditioned consumers to expect unsatisfactory service and goods. 'It created a culture of things that didn't quite fit, didn't quite suit and didn't quite serve,' he says. 'Consumers have become restricted by what machines can make.'

With mass retailing came mass advertising. Without direct contact with the consumer, manufacturers could not know who was buying what; only what was selling. Mass advertising established a link between a product and millions of faceless consumers. Brands – encapsulating a short, memorable message – were part of this relationship. The result has in many cases been fantastically successful: Coca-Cola has created a drink that is instantly recognised and even has emotional resonance.

Yet branding is, at best, an imprecise art. Most consumers would be hard-pressed to explain why, say, Levi's or Nike are losing cachet to such newcomers as Tommy Hilfiger. Because they sell through huge retailers, producers struggle to know why customers buy their brands. 'Manufacturers make things for a buyer called inventory,' says Mr Wunderman. 'They have become separated from the consumer by distributors, wholesalers and retailers.'

As advertising costs have risen and the media have fragmented, mass marketing has become harder and more costly. That, plus new computer technology, has pushed direct marketing into the limelight. Its full potential is only just being grasped. By manipulating information, including data over the Internet, direct marketing can be targeted and personalised. It can even be intelligent – learning what customers like from what they buy and where they browse, as well as soliciting feedback via the telephone and e-mail. The result can be more effective than mass advertising.

The low costs of direct marketing have created a huge and fast-growing industry – made up of direct mail, telemarketing, database marketing, the Internet and free-phone TV, radio and print advertisements. In its biggest market, North America, the industry was worth $163bn in 1998, when it grew by seven per cent to almost three-fifths of the country's total spending on advertising. The industry expects seven per cent annual growth to 2002, beating the 5.5 per cent forecast for advertising spending.

Direct marketing is growing even faster in places where junk mail is new enough still to be welcome. Robert Wientzen, president of America's Direct Marketing Association, says that in Russia and the Czech Republic most junk mail is opened and read – indeed the average piece is pored over by more than one person. Even in China, despite an unreliable postal service and few credit cards, the government is encouraging direct marketing, partly to stop people migrating to cities in search of things to buy.

Yet most direct marketing remains clumsy. Britain's Direct Marketing Association admits its members spend £30 000 ($49 000) a year sending mailings to dead people; typical success rates for most mailshot campaigns in mature countries are not better than 2 per cent. Steve Dapper, chief executive of Rapp Collins, a big direct-marketing agency, complains that consumer data are sold too freely, leading to pesky cold calls and junk mail. The trouble is that direct marketing is still driven by the same thinking as mass marketing.

Most direct marketing is based on profiles built by classification systems that use a mixture of census data, questionnaires, electoral-roll information and, in America, credit-card data to segment populations. This information is passed to a direct-marketing agency to slice into profiles. Having defined a type, the agency buys the names and addresses of similar people from mailing lists sold by list brokers.

The profiles are not sophisticated. Scott Adams, creator of the Dilbert cartoons, jokes that the most important category is 'The Stupid Rich', so named because of their tendency to buy anything that's new, regardless of cost or usefulness. If you sell enough to them, he says, you can afford to sell the rest to 'The Stupid Poor'. One British agency has a database divided into 'Green Wellies' (favoured footwear for country gents, for the uninitiated) and 'Fools and Horses', after a television programme.

These profiles, based on guesswork, are crude. Direct marketers are developing fancier ways to pull narrower consumer segments from databases, using powerful new statistical techniques. Yet, though refining the profiles has improved hit rates, Peter Rosenwalk, founder of Saatchi & Saatchi Direct World-wide and now head of direct marketing at Abril, a Brazilian media group, says better segmentation is still based on old assumptions: 'the most dangerous word in direct marketing is "average". This is still mass advertising – a smaller "mass", but mass advertising.'

Smart companies are trying to circumvent this by gathering information first-hand from customers. Double-click, an American Internet advertising company, sends specific advertisements to people as they browse the web, depending on where they are, the time of day and what they are looking at. These advertisements can produce response rates of over 25 per cent. Others, such as Tesco, a British supermarket, analyse electronic point-of-sale information as people shop, making it possible to change prices at different times of day or to tailor selections to suit local customers.

Yet many companies are still failing to put the information they collect to good use. In Britain WH Smith, a book retailer, gives all customers discounts through a loyalty card, but it collects no data on them. Edwina Dunn of Dunnhumby, the British agency behind Tesco's loyalty scheme, gives a warning about the current fashion for databases: 'If you set up a database, have a question in mind. Otherwise don't do it.'

We're going to have a revolution

Now direct marketing is on the threshold of something new. At its heart is a change in relations between customers and businesses, so that each customer is treated differently. According to Mr Peppers and Ms Rogers, firms must do three things: track what each customer buys, talk to him, and tailor products especially for him.

The key to the first two is to set up a 'learning relationship' with your best customers. This improves with every transaction, defining the customer's needs and tastes in increasing detail. Computers and databases provide foolproof memory for this – every preference can be registered. British Airways greets frequent flyers with their favourite drink and newspaper, based on previous choices. The airline not only expects to gain more satisfied customers; it hopes to reduce stocks and wastage on board. Amazon.com, an online bookseller, recommends books to customers based on past choices. 1–800 Flowers will keep a list of important birthdays for you and even remind you of what you bought last time.

Most enterprises will not be able to treat all their customers so well: it is too expensive. The trick is to identify valuable customers and to concentrate on them, while holding back on or even shedding less profitable ones. This may sound anathema to traditional marketers. But Ms Rogers says she knows of one mid-Western bank in America where less than a third of customers accounted for over 100 per cent of the profits, while the bottom 30 per cent, which it is ditching, actually cost it money.

Similarly, one big Texan computer maker is gently 'firing' service-intensive customers by sending them rivals' models instead of its own; and one British direct-insurance company is seeking to forward calls from high-risk customers to a competitor. Though Telstra, an Australian telecoms company, is not allowed to refuse anyone a telephone connection, it is using its database to sell additional services to its most costly customers – young adults who often move house and want frequent billing cost three times as much as older ones.

Mass customisation is the next step. Dell and Gateway have changed the way computers are sold by allowing customers to configure their own systems, by telephone or over the Internet, and simply shipping them the box. The result is paying off. Dell, which offers over 10,000 computer configurations, is growing at five times the rate of its rivals. By getting workers to build each computer to order, Dell also keeps fewer stocks.

Similarly, Levi Strauss is introducing web-linked kiosks in its stores, where customers can design their own pair of jeans, choosing from a number of styles, colours, shapes and sizes. The information is instantly related to its Tennessee factory, where the jeans are cut individually. To improve quality and reduce errors, each pair of jeans is made from start to finish by a single group of workers. Another example is Japan's National Bicycle Company, which turns out bikes in any size, colour or style without any increase in costs or delivery time.

Traditional retailers and manufacturers may feel uneasy about the way direct marketing is going. A switch from product-led to consumer-led marketing, in which individual tastes matter, gives an in-built advantage to small, flexible companies. Although large retailers will own a lot of detailed information, many of the expensive assets they have built up may become obsolete – especially as cheaper distribution channels such as the Internet gain ground. Some big manufacturers may have to revert from mass production to customised production.

Winners and losers

Direct, personalised marketing also raises doubts about brands. By definition, bespoke goods are hard to brand. Mr Wunderman argues that, as mass customisation becomes feasible, each customer becomes, in effect, his own brand. Julia Groves, manager of British Airways' digital marketing, adds that brands will come to be associated not with what a product does or with the type of services on offer, but with service quality.

However, direct marketing may raise concerns about privacy, as companies learn more about the habits of their individual clients. The Federal Trade Commission recently gave a warning that a mere 2 per cent of websites have a comprehensive privacy policy. Privacy is a legitimate concern, as most direct marketers already recognise. On both sides of the Atlantic, consumers are usually given access to data about themselves so that they can correct it; and they also have the option to refuse to allow data to be transferred to third parties. The argument between Europe and America is not about these principles, but how to enforce them. The EU does it through legislation; the Americans, mindful of the risk of stifling marketing innovation, prefer to rely on voluntary self-regulation.

Yet the most effective protection for privacy may be commercial pressure. As selling shifts from seeking new customers to retaining existing ones, businesses will recognise both the cost of alienating customers through clumsy and unsolicited marketing and the benefit of good service. Increasingly they will seek customers' permission before marketing to them. Businesses that use data to deliver better service to customers while also respecting their privacy will be the real winners in the direct-market revolution.

Source: The Economist, 9 January 1999

Illustration 7.3 below details the attempts by two manufacturers to utilize the Internet in new areas of business. Consider Sony first. Remember we looked briefly at Sony in Chapter 1 when we discussed the diverse nature of the media industry. Here is one of the world's best known and most innovative companies moving into Internet banking, that is, offering a new product to existing and new customers. At one level, the move appears to be similar to those of leading retailers such as Marks & Spencer and Tesco moving into financial services. However, as the article points out, the twin drivers are Sony's need to raise its profile as an Internet company, and also the exploitation of the shake-up in Japan's financial sector. Also, this move would strengthen the networking aspects of Sony's business which may play an important role in the future. The move of Intel into supplying a range of consumer web appliances is also of interest. This would mark the first time that the company, a manufacturer of microchips for PCs, had attempted to manufacture and sell consumer products as opposed to being a supplier of a crucial element in a product (you may recall that we looked at the PC industry in Chapter 3).

The moves outlined by these two companies below provides some evidence that the scope for the Internet outlined by Ghosh was at least partly accurate. Here we have Sony offering a new product and Intel moving to offer web appliances in a way that neither had done before. In both cases we can see examples of Sony and Intel designing and delivering new products to customers. Both are also trying to develop direct links to customers and Intel is almost certainly endeavouring to bypass competitors in the value chain. We should note that not all manufacturers' moves to create a direct relationship with their end consumers have been successful. For example, Levi Strauss, the famous manufacturer of jeans and casual clothing, was unable to make a success of its Internet operations, claiming that it would seek to collaborate with an established retailer who understood consumers better than it did as a manufacturer.

Illustration 7.3

Sony Moves into Internet Banking

Sony, inventor of the Walkman and the Playstation video games machine, plans to diversify into internet banking nine months after setting up a joint venture online brokerage firm.

The move conforms with Sony's strategy of raising its profile as an internet company and exploiting the shake-up of Japan's financial sector. Other non-finance companies have already made forays into the financial services arena.

Ito-Yokado, one of Japan's biggest supermarket operators, and Softbank, the internet and media company, are part of a consortium that has submitted a bid to buy Nippon Credit Bank, which was nationalised last year.

Softbank's aim is to develop an internet conglomerate centred on financial services and Ito-Yokado plans to offer banking services through its outlets, which include Seven-Eleven Japan.

In following suit, Sony is expanding its digital media platform 'Will Sony become a supplier of personal finance? You bet 100 per cent we will,' said Nobuyuki Idei, its president, in a recent Financial Times interview.

The group, which already has insurance and finance subsidiaries, intends to establish an online banking service by summer 2001, offering individuals loans, savings and billpaying services.

It is considering capitalising the internet bank at ¥20bn (£120m) with the aim of collecting ¥1000bn in deposits within the first five years.

'Sony is trying to reinforce its financial business and strengthen its brand image to be able to compete better in the digital market,' said Masashi Kubota, consumer electronics analyst at ING Baring Securities.

'It also wants to reinforce its networking operations. It has a strong hardware and contents business and the only area it is weak in is networking. Right now, strengthening the networking business is its main theme.'

Intel to launch 'web appliances'

Intel, the world's largest semiconductor maker, plans to launch a range of consumer 'web appliances' – computer-like devices giving high-speed internet access.

The simple-to-use machines, the cornerstone of a strategy designed to extend the use of Intel technology, will be powered by the company's Celeron microprocessors.

Unlike general purpose personal computers capable of a wide range of tasks, web appliances perform limited tasks over the internet such as e-mail retrieval, information gathering or online shopping.

Some may look like slimmed-down PCs while others will be designed for use in specific places, for example the kitchen or in a car. They are likely to be provided 'free' with a subscription service, for uses such as home shopping or online banking.

In a surprise decision, to help keep prices down, the machines will run the 'open source' Line operating system software rather than Microsoft Windows, which powers most personal computers. Intel will outline its web appliance strategy today at the Consumer Electronics Show in Las Vegas.

The strategy involves providing software and services to suppliers as well as the hardware itself.

'We see a significant business opportunity to bring the internet to new devices in the home,' said Claude Leglise, vice president of Intel architecture business group and general manager of the company's home products group.

'Our strategy focuses on providing telecom operators and service providers with a cost-effective platform on which they can offer their services and remotely manage the new appliances,' he said.

Mr Leglise dismissed suggestions that the launch of web appliances might reduce sales of Intel-chip powered PCs. 'They are two different markets,' he said, emphasising that the PC was seen as a general purpose machine while web appliances would be designed for specific functions.

The machines are expected to incorporate hard drives for storage and fast internet access technology such as ADSL (asymmetric digital subscriber line) or cable modems and will include smartcard capabilities in Europe.

Intel's first web appliances should be available in mid-2000 and will integrate internet access with telephony features such as call management, e-mails and faxes.

The US group said it was working with telecom operators, internet service providers and e-commerce retailers worldwide to launch services using its new machines. These include NEC's BiGlobe in Japan, USWest, and LASER-Galeries Lafayette in France.

Source: Financial Times, 11 December 1999 and 20 January 2000

Although much of the publicity relates to 'business to consumer' commerce by far the largest number and value of transactions takes place business to business. A recent report by consultants Price Waterhouse Coopers noted not only the significant growth in internet connections (up to 83 per cent of companies in 1998) but also significant electronic data interchange (EDI) interactions between customers and suppliers. The report noted that e-business technologies have been deployed extensively in the automotive, consumer goods and technology industries. Most executives in the automotive industry believe that the implementation of e-business is crucial to being world-class. The report goes on to note that there were significant reductions in customer lead-time as a consequence of e-business developments. In Chapter 5 we examined some of the latest developments in supply chain management and Illustration 7.4 below builds on some of those themes. This example identifies in broad terms how the car industry is seeking to use Internet technologies not only to manage the supply chain better but also to remove significant costs. You may also recall that we came across this industry in Chapter 6. This example is significant because it indicates how car makers may collaborate in order to exert pressure on their suppliers. The savings appear to be significant, and car makers appear willing to collaborate not only with direct competitors, but also with other firms with necessary complementary skills and resources (Oracle and Cisco). It does appear that this is yet another example of how suppliers to an industry can have their bargaining power significantly reduced.

Illustration 7.4

Nissan May Join Ford Buying Pool

Carlos Ghosn, Nissan's chief operating officer, revealed on Tuesday the company had been invited by Oracle, the US software group, to join the e-commerce, business-to-business venture set up with Ford Motor Company.

Mr Ghosn said that the proposal was under review, along with another proposition. And he indicated that if Nissan decided to join the Ford-Oracle trade exchange – which aims to save hundreds of millions of dollars by allowing manufacturers to pool purchasing on the internet – France's Renault, and its sizeable supply base, would probably join as well. Renault acquired a large minority stake in Nissan last year.

Mr Ghosn, who was sent in by the French carmaker to sort out Nissan's troubled and heavily indebted business, sounded relatively upbeat about the response of suppliers to Nissan's call for cost cuts.

The company is looking for 20 per cent cost reductions, but offering more extensive relationships in return. Suppliers are expected to finalise proposals this month and Mr Ghosn said decisions on new contracts should be made by the beginning of April.

Mr Ghosn cautioned that, out of the three key targets for success outlined by the company last year, the goal of moving into the black in the current year would be the toughest to achieve. In the event of failure, Mr Ghosn added, the entire executive committee would resign.

Mr Ghosn also indicated that the situation at Nissan Diesel was progressing, although he conceded that resolving the capital structure and stabilising the business had taken longer than some expected.

The company was examining expressions of interest in the heavy truck business, in which Nissan Motors holds a 22 per cent stake, but no decision was likely until these issues were resolved – which could happen 'in a matter of weeks'.

The Ford-Oracle business-to-business joint venture was unveiled in November, as was a similar plan from General Motors and Commerce One.

The extended supply chain at Ford alone is valued at about $300bn, which analysts estimate could provide the joint venture with revenues of $4bn-$5bn within five years.

From the outset, the partners indicated they were likely to invite other manufacturers to utilise the technology, thus increasing the revenue stream and spreading potential savings.

This week Alice Miles, president of Ford's B2B, said the joint venture hoped to be able to announce that another carmaker would join the system in the first half of 2000.

CISCO: Communications Manufacturer in Venture with Carmakers

Cisco Systems, the US communications equipment manufacturer that on Wednesday overtook General Electric to become the world's second most highly valued company, is joining AutoXchange, the e-commerce venture set up last year by Ford Motor Company and Oracle.

Ford, the second-largest carmaker, and Oracle, the software group, said Cisco would take an undisclosed equity stake in AutoXchange and provide 'kits' to help dealers and suppliers connect to the system. The kits will be offered at an 'affordable price' to entitles seeking to join AutoXchange, although the companies said there would be no obligation to utilise the Cisco package.

Ford also said it recently completed its first parts procurement auction on the system. It said the value of the particular production item sourced was $78m and that about five 'tier-one' suppliers had been involved in bidding on the business.

Ford said the savings – compared with the traditional procurement cost – had run to double-digits, and that the part in question was one 'used in every car'. It refused to elaborate further, citing the desire to protect supplier privacy.

The carmaker added that it expected to hold further auctions for about $300m of supply business in February. It said there had been 'a lot of progress' in efforts to entice other carmakers to join AutoXchange.

Ford and General Motors announced rival e-commerce ventures last year, and have been battling to woo both suppliers and other car makers onto these systems.

The ventures are significant within the burgeoning e-commerce area because of the scale of supply chains within the car industry. Ford's direct purchasing requirement totals about $80bn a year, and it has more than 30 000 suppliers.

Both groups are hoping the e-business systems can be used for their own purchasing and by suppliers. However, some suppliers have expressed reservations and appear to fear that they will be forced to choose between the Ford and GM networks, and that these could lead to a further squeeze on costs.

Source: Financial Times, 20 January 2000 and 10 February 2000

7.3 Concluding Thoughts

Throughout this book we have sought, through considering real companies and real events, to enhance our understanding of how competition works for consumers and suppliers. In general we have eschewed oversimplistic prescriptions and relied instead on a rigorous analysis of the issues under discussion. However, having done all that, we will now spend just a few moments in speculating about the changes that are likely to happen in the future. Here we are guided not only by what has happened in the past and by events that are already under way, but also by our understanding of organizations and their customers.

Most commentators would argue that the rate of change is likely to accelerate. We can think of changes to how goods and services are produced now and how they are likely to be developed and delivered in the future. We would hope, in what we have written so far, that nevertheless there are some enduring lessons. For example, the rate of change in information and communications technology (ICT), and firms' and individuals' ability to access and use it, are going to change the way that most goods and services are marketed and delivered. But before we explore this in a little more detail we should remember that historically we have lived through other significant, possibly more significant, changes such as the advent of railways, canals, telephones and telex to name a few, which were momentous events in the nineteenth century which changed the way that goods and services were developed. We believe that there are two major related developments that will change the way that all organizations compete and the way that we as customers and consumers behave. We have dealt with the first, developments in ICTs, at length already in this chapter but it is also linked to the second development, globalization, which we referred to earlier (Chapters 1 and 5 in particular).

These two phenomena together are likely to reshape the way in which firms not only compete with each other but also therefore the way in which they work themselves. For example, we have already demonstrated that firms, if they are to compete effectively, will have to develop sophisticated global supply chains and associated logistics capabilities to manage these networks. They will have to grapple again, therefore, with issues of centralization or decentralization. Fragmenting consumer choice on the one hand will be a formidable force for decentralization; but common ICT systems and global sourcing and supply chains will be a countervailing force for centralization, or shared services as it is becoming known. The speed of communication using the net coupled with on-line integrated ERP systems providing almost minute by minute status reports on what is happening, plus the need to maximize purchasing clout, leads us to conclude that the centre will retain authority for global supply deals.

One consequence of this is that we would expect to see firms accelerate the trend whereby they seek to shape and influence consumer preferences. It is instructive and illustrative to think of the amount of money spent by the new Dot.com companies to create demand for their services and products, as opposed to the proportion they spend on investing in their infrastructure or product. This leads us to another aspect, which is likely to change, and that is the growth of intermediaries, or infomediaries in the wired world. We noted earlier in this chapter (Figure 7.1) that most goods and services sold over the Internet are high in search or experience qualities. So in order to sell using that medium, firms would need to develop technologies such that their services were viewed by customers as having a high level of search or experience attributes. This would apply to both the supplier of the service or the intermediary acting on their behalf – such as an auction web site or other form of e-tailer.

For consumers the increasing variety on offer in the future may seem very tempting. The trend to increasing globalization and reliability of ICT networks means that, theoretically at least, we can buy goods from anywhere in the world. The main proviso is that such purchases conform first to our own preferences and perceptions in terms of quality, price and value, and second that we have confidence in the firm/outlet/website from whom we are purchasing. It is the latter point that is most important and explains why, for example, traditional manufacturers and retailers (such as Bosch, Sony, Marks & Spencer, Barnes & Noble) are seeking to protect and project their own reputations and brands on to the Internet as reliable trusted suppliers. The other issue here relates to the regulations under which such transactions take place. Do the laws of the UK, US, Germany or wherever apply should the consumer seek redress for faulty goods or services? Since consumers are, if they wish, operating in a global market there may well be a role for national governments and international agencies in regulating this environment to ensure that not only is competition free from distortion, but also that the consumer has adequate protection.

References and Further Reading

Albert, M. (1993). *Capitalism against Capitalism*. London: Whurr.

Asch, D., Segal-Horn, S. and Suneja V. (1998). 'Signalling Product Quality as an Element in Business Strategy: Conceptual Issues and Empirical Evidence'. The *18th Annual Strategic Management Society Conference*, Florida.

Assael, H. (1984). *Consumer Behaviour and Marketing Action,* 2nd edn. Boston, MA: Kent Publishing.

Bowman, C. and Asch, D. (1987). *Strategic Management*. Basingstoke: Macmillan.

Bowman, C. and Asch, D. (1996). *Managing Strategy*. Basingstoke: Macmillan.

Brown, S. L. and Eisenhardt, K. M. (1998). *Competing on the Edge*. Boston, MA: Harvard Business School Press.

Brush, T. H. and Artz, K. W. (1999). 'Toward a Contingent Resource-Based Theory: The Information Asymmetry on the Value of Capabilities in Veterinary Medicine'. *Strategic Management Journal*, 20: 223–50.

Christensen, C. M. and Tedlow, R. S. (2000). Patterns of Disruption in Retailing. *Harvard Business Review,* Jan-Feb: 42–5.

Czerniawska, F. and Potter, G. (1998). *Business in a Virtual World*. Basingstoke: Macmillan.

Darby, M. R. and Karni, E. (1973). 'Free Competition and the Optimal Amount of Fraud'. *Journal of Law and Economics,* 16 (April): 67–86.

De Kare-Silver, M. (1998). *e-shock*. Basingstoke: Macmillan.

De Kare-Silver, M. (2000). *e-shock 2000*. Basingstoke: Macmillan.

Deneckere, R. J. and McAfee, R. P. (1996). 'Damaged Goods'. *Journal of Economics & Management Strategy,* 5(2): 149–74.

Dobson, P. and Waterson, M. (1999). 'Retailer Power: How Regulators Should Respond to Greater Concentration in Retailing'. *Economic Policy,* 28 (April): 135–164.

Dunne, D. and Narasimhan, C. (1999). 'The New Appeal of Private Labels'. *Harvard Business Review,* May-June: 41–52.

Ghosh, S. (1998). 'Making Business Sense of the Internet'. *Harvard Business Review,* March-April: 126–35.

Gray, J. (1998). *False Dawn.* London: Granta.

Hagel, J. I. and Singer, M. (1999). *Net Worth.* Boston, MA: Harvard Business School Press.

Harvey, M. (1999). 'Innovation and Competition in UK Supermarkets'. *Briefing Paper 3, ESRC Centre for Research on Innovation and Competition.*

Heilbroner, R. and Thurow, L. (1998). *Economics Explained.* New York: Simon & Schuster.

Kay, J. (1996). *The Business of Economics.* Oxford: Oxford University Press.

Magretta, J. (1998) The Power of Virtual Integration: An Interview with Dell Computer's Michael Dell. *Harvard Business Review,* March-April.

Nelson, P. (1970). 'Information and Consumer Behaviour'. *Journal of Political Economy,* 78: 311–29.

Nelson, P. (1974). 'Advertising as Information'. *Journal of Political Economy,* 81: 729–54.

Peters, T. and Waterman, W. (1982). *In Search of Excellence.* London: Harper & Row.

Peters, T. (1987). *Thriving on Chaos,* New York: Knopf.

Peters, T. (1992). *Liberation Management.* London: Macmillan.

Piel, G. (1992). *Only One World.* New York, W.H. Freeman.

Porter, M. E. (1980). *Competitive Strategy:Techniques for Analysing Industries and Competitors.* New York: Free Press.

Shapiro, C. and Varian, H. R. (1999). *Information Rules.* Boston, MA: Harvard Business School Press.

Simonson, I. and Tversky, A. (1992). 'Choice in Context: Tradeoff Contrast and Extremeness Aversion'. *Journal of Marketing Research,* 29 (August): 281–95.

Smith, G. E. and Nagle, T. T. (1995). 'Frames of Reference and Buyers' Perception of Price and Value.' *California Management Review,* 38(1): 98–116.

Tapscott, D. (1996). *The Digital Economy: Promise and Peril in the Age of Networked Intelligence.* New York: McGraw-Hill.

Thomas, H. and T. Pollock (1999). 'From I-O Economics S-C-P Paradigm througjh Strategic Groups to Competence-Based Competition: Reflections on the Puzzle of Competitive Strategy'. *British Journal of Management,* 10(2): 127–40.

Wolfe, B. S. and Asch, D. (1992). 'Retailers Squeeze Electric Appliance Manufacturers'. *Long Range Planning,* 25(74): 102–09.

Wolfe, B. S. (1996) 'The Development of the UK Domestic Electrical Industry from 1964 to 1990', unpublished MPhil. dissertation, The Open University.

Zeithaml, V. A. and Bitner, M. J. (1996). *Services Marketing*. New York: McGraw-Hill.

Index